Along the Erie Canal

With the Municipal Seals of the Cities, Towns and Villages of New York

Erie Canal Bicentennial Edition

Compiled by Marvin W. Bubie

Square Circle Press
Schenectady, New York

Along the Erie Canal
With the Municipal Seals of the Cities,
Towns and Villages of New York

Published by
Square Circle Press LLC
PO Box 913
Schenectady, New York 12301
www.squarecirclepress.com

©2010, 2017 by Marvin W. Bubie.
All rights reserved. No part of this publication may be reproduced or transmitted in any form or by any means, electronic or mechanical, except brief quotes extracted for the purpose of book reviews or similar articles, without permission in writing from the publisher.

First edition 2010, privately published.
Erie Canal Bicentennial Edition, 2017.
Printed and bound in the United States of America on acid-free, durable paper.
ISBN 13: 978-0-9989670-0-4
ISBN 10: 0-9989670-0-9
Library of Congress Control Number: 2017940910

Cover design by Richard Vang, ©2017, Square Circle Press. Front cover: Photograph of boat exiting lock, courtesy of Marvin Bubie.

Title page: "Historic Clifton Park: The Erie Canal at Vischer Ferry," by Christi Vadnais. Image with permission of the artist. The mural is installed in the Clifton Park Center Mall. The image has been altered for use on the title page.

Notice: After due diligence, the author and publisher were unable to discover any information on the artist or the title of the illustration used on page 79. The publisher respectfully requests that any interested party please contact us with any pertinent information. The caption will be corrected and proper credit given, or if requested, the illustration will be removed, in any subsequent editions of this book.

This book is dedicated to my parents, William and Eleanor Bubie, whose faith in me never wavered and without whom I could not have succeeded in my quests or imagined that I should try. They encouraged my love of books and imbued all of their children with a strong sense of family that extends beyond kin to a larger brotherhood and a sense of history that connects us with the past. Their wise counsel—and more importantly the example of their lives—has and still does serve me well in my life.

They encouraged me to go to the very expensive Rensselaer Polytechnic Institute, with the philosophy that if I got the grades, they would help in getting the money, although no one knew exactly how. It is thoroughly American to begin a large ambitious project without knowing all the details of how to complete it.

Visionaries like DeWitt Clinton and Stephen Van Rensselaer saw the Erie Canal filling a need in the country without knowing how long it would take. The engineers Benjamin Wright, Canvass White, and Amos Eaton, without formal engineering training or experience, designed and built the canal against much opposition and skepticism. Together they ushered in a new industrial age for our country.

I am forever grateful to my parents for living the dream this country made possible and for passing on that lesson.

Contents

Preface, vii

Introduction, *3*
City of Buffalo, *5*
Niagara County, *6*
City of Tonawanda, *7*
City of North Tonawanda, *8*
Town of Pendleton, *9*
Town of Lockport, *10*
City of Lockport, *11*
Town of Royalton, *12*
Village of Middleport, *13*
Orleans County, *14*
Town of Ridgeway, *15*
Village of Medina, *16*
Town of Kendall, *17*
Village of Holley, *18*
Village of Brockport, *19*
Town of Ogden, *20*
Village of Spencerport, *21*
City of Rochester, *22*
Village of Pittsford, *23*
Town of Perinton, *24*
Village of Fairport, *25*

Wayne County, *26*
Town of Macedon, *27*
Village of Macedon, *28*
Town of Palmyra, *29*
Town of Arcadia, *30*
Town of Lyons, *31*
Village of Clyde, *32*
Town of Montezuma, *33*
Village of Port Byron, *34*
Village of Weedsport, *35*
Village of Jordan, *36*
Town of Elbridge, *37*
Village of Liverpool, *38*
City of Syracuse, *39*
Village of Chittenango, *40*
Village of Canastota, *41*
Oneida County, *42*
Village of Sylvan Beach, *43*
Town of Verona, *44*
City of Rome, *45*
Village of Whitesboro, *46*
City of Utica, *47*

Village of Frankfort, *48*
Village of Ilion, *49*
City of Little Falls, *50*
Town of St. Johnsville, *51*
Village of Fultonville, *52*
City of Amsterdam, *54*
Schenectady County, *55*
Town of Rotterdam, *56*
Town of Glenville, *57*
City of Schenectady, *58*
Town of Niskayuna, *59*
Town of Clifton Park, *60*
City of Cohoes, *61*
The Great Cohoes Falls, *62*
Town of Waterford, *63*
City of Troy, *64*
Rensselaer Polytechnic Institute, *65*
City of Watervliet, *66*
Village of Menands, *67*
City of Albany, *68*
New York City, *69*

Appendix 1: Other Canals in New York State, 70
Appendix 2: Notable Men of the Erie Canal, 72
Appendix 3: Inventions from the Erie Canal, 77
Appendix 4: The Erie Canal as Subject for Works of Art, 80
Appendix 5: Erie Canal Museums in New York State, 83
Appendix 6: Erie Canal Envy in the U.S., 92

Acknowledgments, 130
About the Author, 134

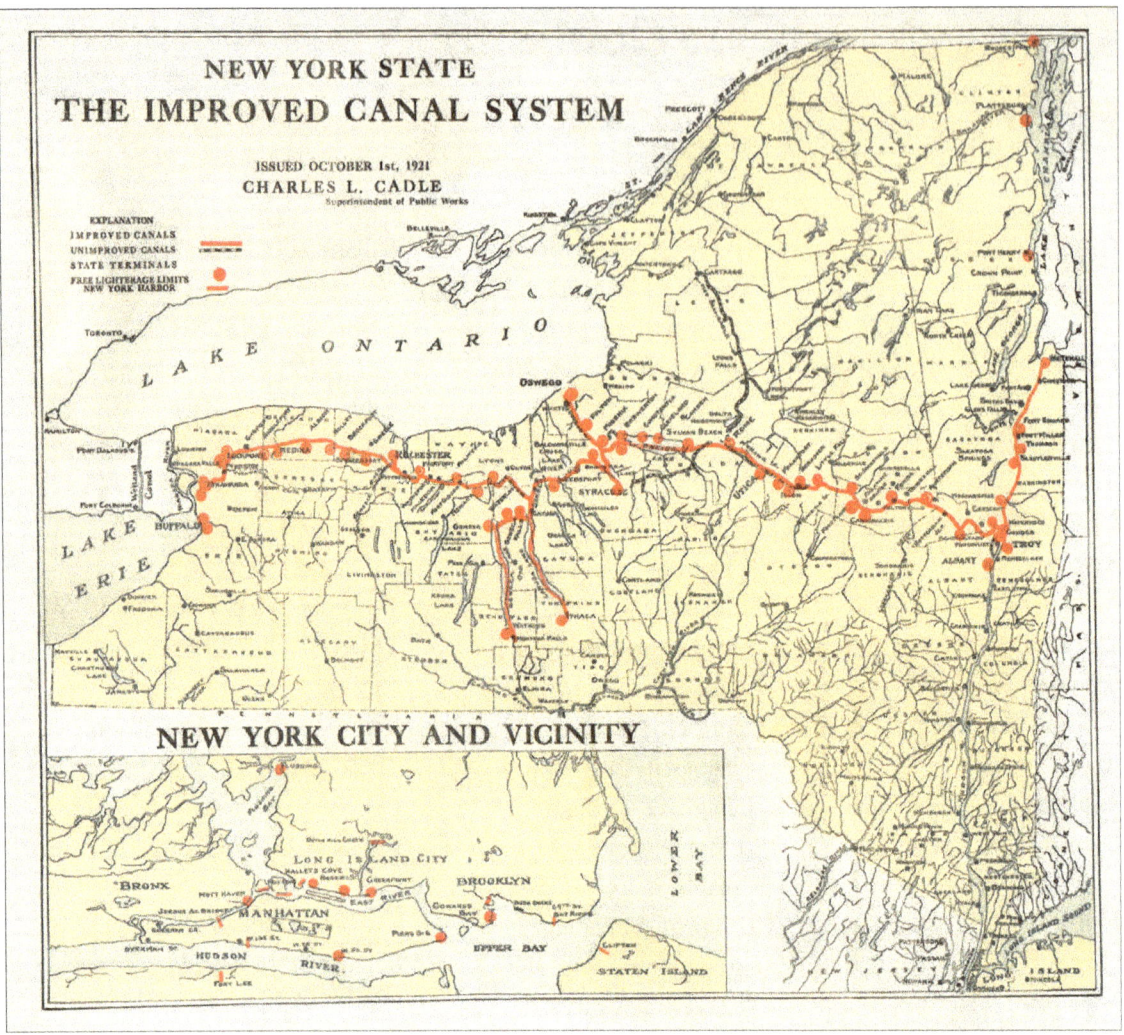

This 1921 map of the Improved Barge Canal System shows the route of the Erie Canal from Buffalo to Albany and the cities, towns and villages along it, as well as the other, later canals extending north and south. However, it can be argued that from the opening of the canal in 1825, the city that was impacted the most was New York City.

Preface

My hobby has been the collection and study of municipal seals. My interest in municipal seals in the United States stems from the fact that "We the People" get to determine the seals of our communities. Seals are a form of self identification. The seals of the municipalities along the Erie Canal in New York State indicate that their identity is intertwined with the canal. 200 years after it was built, the canal is experiencing a rebirth as a source of tourism and recreation, with annual festivals and reinvestment in areas that border the canal. The number of museums along the canal indicates the continuing interest in its heritage.

Many of the descriptions of the municipalities and their seals are from their own websites, their municipal historians or their own municipal codes. The Erie Canal is the history they have chosen to commemorate on their municipal buildings, vehicles, podiums and letterheads. With relatively few exceptions of those municipalities that were established prior to 1817, this collection of seals reflects the continuing importance of the Erie Canal.

The new edition of this book includes not only a collection of seals along the Erie Canal, but also in the appendices some example seals of municipalities along other canals in New York and other states that followed New York's lead ("canal envy"). The seals along the Erie Canal are presented from west to east; the others are gathered together by state and follow an alphabetical sequence by state.

The inclusion of any municipal seal or logo does not imply endorsement of this book in any way. In addition, many of the seals included are protected by copyright and permission was required prior to their use. And, unfortunately, a good clear image was not always obtainable or did not even exist for some municipalities. In other cases, the official seal is black and white, but a color seal is used on municipal vehicles and the like, and which are usually much more interesting to see. In all cases, the best available images were used in this book.

In addition to the seals from other states with canals, this new addition includes information in the appendices that supplement the history presented in the seals from New York State.

Marvin Bubie
2010, revised 2017

Along the Erie Canal

Introduction

The Erie Canal was one of the defining projects of this country. It ranks in importance with the completion of the transcontinental railroad in 1869, the building of the interstate highway system begun in the 1950s and the moon landing in 1969. Each had a dramatic and lasting effect on the country as a whole.

Begun on July 4, 1817 in Rome, New York and completed on October 26, 1825, the 363-mile Erie Canal was the longest canal built in the United States, stretching from Buffalo to Albany, and connecting the Hudson River to Lake Erie. It was financed and owned by the State of New York. When the Erie Canal was completed in 1825, it promised a cheap and efficient means of transporting goods to market. Many marveled at the canal, calling it the "Eighth Wonder of the World."

The original canal was 40 feet wide and 4 feet deep, limiting the size and number of boats used. It was an engineering triumph completed largely without engineers. It became the first "school" of engineering for the country and led directly to the founding of Rensselaer Polytechnic Institute by Stephen Van Rensselaer. Visionaries like DeWitt Clinton had to persist in the face of opposition by those who did not believe it could be accomplished at all.

Large numbers of immigrants came to build the canal without machinery. Although many nationalities participated, the Irish comprised the largest percentage. One answer to the question of how the canal was built is, "With Yankee ingenuity and Hibernian brawn."

The official opening of the full length of the Erie Canal was on October 26, 1825. When the flotilla of boats left Buffalo, word was "telegraphed" to New York City by the firing of cannons that were placed every five to twelve miles along the route. It took fifty-five minutes for the message to reach New York.

As a milestone in the history of the nation, "Clinton's Ditch" was the Internet of its era, opening new vistas and changing the lives of those who ventured upon its waters. It opened up the western frontier via the Great Lakes, and dramatically reduced the cost of transportation. Literally overnight, the cost of transporting a ton of merchandise dropped from over $120 to less than $8. A six-week trip by horse and wagon was reduced to six days by canal. It was the single reason New York became known as the "Empire State," and for the port of New York City eventually surpassing its rivals of Baltimore, Philadelphia and Boston, all of which were larger at the time of the canal's opening.

Other developments followed, including the establishment of the cities, towns and villages along the length of the canal. The country began its industrialization and left its colonial past behind. Still other social developments followed the route of the canal, the suffragette movement and the Underground Railroad among them.

The canal was enlarged twice, in 1860 and 1909, but with the advent of the railroads, the importance of the Erie Canal as a vital part of the settlement of the Midwest and as a commercial shipping enterprise gradually diminished. To counteract this, between 1905 and 1918 New York State constructed the Barge Canal. It is the direct descendant of the Erie Canal and a network of connecting waterways that have been in continuous operation since 1825. It too, though, has slowly become less used for transportation and more for pleasure craft and tour boats.

Even so, the economic impact today of the New York State Canal System (which includes the currently operating Erie, Champlain, Cayuga-Seneca, and Oswego Canals) is valued at $6.2 billion annually to the state. It provides drinking water to 221,000 people and provides irrigation to farms and golf courses. It is still used to ship goods that are not easily shipped by truck or rail, and the canal still remains the most fuel-efficient way to ship goods between the East Coast and the upper Midwest. One gallon of diesel pulls one ton of cargo 59 miles by truck, 202 miles by train and 514 miles by canal barge. A single barge can carry 3,000 tons, enough to replace 100 trucks.

As the oldest continuously operating canal in the U.S., it is a world-class destination for tourism and recreation. In 2000, the National Parks Service designated the 524 miles of waterway that make up the Canal System, and the more than 200 surrounding canal communities, as the "Erie Canalway National Heritage Corridor."

In recognition of the national significance of America's most iconic, influential and enduring waterway, the New York State Barge Canal was designated as a Historic District on the National Register in October 2014. The designation recognizes the constituent canals of the N.Y.S. Canal System as nationally significant works of early-twentieth century engineering and construction that impacted transportation and maritime commerce for nearly half a century.

City of Buffalo

The Village of Buffalo was originally surveyed in 1804 and incorporated in 1822. It was burned by the British during the War of 1812. The conflict delayed the start of the Erie Canal, and from 1819 until 1822, Buffalo competed with Black Rock to become the western terminus. The completion of the canal ensured Buffalo's future as the "Gateway to the West." The City of Buffalo was granted a charter in 1832. The lighthouse was built in 1833.

From the City Code (*Chapter 44 SEAL/5.44-1. Adoption; description*):

> The Seal of the City of Buffalo heretofore used for that purpose is hereby officially adopted as the City Seal and is described as follows: to the left center, lighthouse on pier; to the right of the lighthouse, ship with three (3) masts showing sails; to the lower right, canal boat drawn by two (2) draft animals proceeding in direction leading toward or past the pier: the above shall be all surrounded by a double circle and between said circles appearing the words "SEAL OF THE CITY OF BUFFALO."

Niagara County

Niagara County was formed from Genesee County in 1808. On April 2, 1821, Niagara County separated from what became Erie County, retaining all lands north of Tonawanda Creek. By this time that area contained the original towns of Niagara, Lewiston, Porter, Wilson, Cambria, Hartland, and Royalton. The main occupation during the early years was subsistence farming.

Lockport witnessed a great influx of Irish immigrants during the 1820s, employed primarily as laborers, for the construction of the Erie Canal. The digging of the canal largely influenced the tremendous growth of Lockport. From 1915 to 1970, North Tonawanda was the home of the world famous Herschell Carrousel Factory. They produced more carousels than other manufacturer.

The seal contains illustrations of America's oldest State Park (1885), Niagara Falls, the famous "Flight of Five" on the Erie Canal, Herschell Carrousel Factory Museum, and a bushel of apples for the abundance of orchards.

City of Tonawanda

Tonawanda is an Indian name meaning "swift water."

The City of Tonanwanda is located alongside the Niagara River and Erie Canal.

The first known settler within the present-day boundaries arrived in 1803. Originally named the Village of Niagara in 1823, it was changed shortly thereafter to the Village of Tonawanda.

The opening of the Erie Canal in 1825 allowed people to move west easily and thus stimulated settlement in the village.

The seal appears to illustrate a Gaff Ketch sailing ship. These were used primarily as passenger ships on the Great Lakes, further transporting the people who arrived on the small packet boats used on the canal.

City of North Tonawanda

Before settlement, this area of Western New York was a land of vast forests and beautiful waterways. The only inhabitants were the Iroquois Indians and a few brave traders. It was the Iroquois who named this area *Tonawanda* after the "swift water" of the Tonawanda Creek.

Because of the birth of the Erie Canal, the area saw a rapid growth in population and jobs. This waterway (that both separates and links the City of Tonawanda and the City of North Tonawanda) was an important factor in the development of the country's commerce back in the mid-1800s. One example was the Wulitzer Company, which was established in North Tonawanda in 1859, partly due to the canal transportation system and partly to the large pool of German-speaking workers.

The seal's nautical anchor denotes the importance of boats and shipping to the city.

Town of Pendleton

The Town of Pendleton extends from the central part of Niagara County to the southern boundary, which is the Tonawanda Creek. The town straddles the Erie Canal.

    The Town of Pendleton was taken from Niagara on February 2, 1824. The town was named after Sylvester Pendleton Clarke, Ex-Governor of Grand Island, the largest island in the Niagara River.

    The seal illustrates the silhouette of the town and its self-described motto as a "Country Community on the Canal."

Town of Lockport

The state legislature passed an act in 1816 which convinced land speculators that the proposed Erie Canal would pass through the area now known as Lockport.

The town itself was established in 1824, the same year the canal was completed from the Hudson River to the foot of the locks. Western freight was portaged to Pendleton and reloaded on boats. The actual locks were the most difficult portion of the canal and had yet to be completed.

On June 6, 1825, General Lafayette paid a four-hour visit to Lockport and received a hero's welcome. On October 26, the full length of the Erie Canal was opened. On that day Governor DeWitt Clinton came through Lockport aboard the *Seneca Chief* and passed successfully through the twin flight of locks.

The Town of Lockport surrounds the City of Lockport which was created in 1865. The logo was adopted in the mid-1980s as a result of a contest. The rising sun is illustrative of the bright future of the town.

City of Lockport

Settled in 1816, Lockport is a city that quite literally grew from the banks of the Erie Canal.

Lockport sits on top of a massive ridge of solid rock known as the Niagara Escarpment, the same prehistoric geology that created Niagara Falls. The countryside to the east of Lockport rests 70 feet below. This rise was the dilemma faced by contractors of the Erie Canal in 1822. An engineering marvel of the time was proposed and built, a double set of five locks, five ascending and five descending the Niagara Escarpment. It was designed by Nathan Roberts of Canastota (see page 75).

On October 26, 1825 the full length of the Erie Canal was opened. On that day Governor DeWitt Clinton came through Lockport aboard the *Seneca Chief* and descended successfully through the twin flight of locks.

The seal illustrates the famous "Flight of Five."

Town of Royalton

The first settlement within the limits of this town was the result of an accident, if tradition may be believed. In 1800, Joshua Slaton was on his way from Vermont to Canada with his family when his wagon broke down. What he saw of this locality during his necessary delay pleased him and he took up land in the northwest corner of the town, cleared a part of it, and built a log house. The Town of Royalton was charted in 1817, the same year that work began in Rome on the Erie Canal.

The Village of Middleport and the hamlets of Gasport, Orangeport, and South Royalton in this town were mostly brought into existence by the construction of the canal. When it was opened, business interests rapidly gathered where Middleport stands.

Mrs. Mabel Hass of Middleport created the winning design of the seal for a contest in 1976 sponsored by the Royalton Bicentennial Committee. It features a barge on the Erie Canal, migrating geese, and a rural farm scene.

Village of Middleport

The Village of Middleport takes its name from being located mid-way between Lockport and Albion. The Board of Trustees adopted the official crest of the village on March 16, 2009.

"A Friendly Community" was adopted decades ago as the village's motto following a visit to the village by President Franklin D. Roosevelt. The story is that when he stopped there, he claimed Middleport looked like "a friendly community." The buildings represent the Village Hall, the Police Department, and other buildings adjoining them on Main Street.

The canal represents the historic Erie Barge Canal, which passes through the middle of the village. The tree represents the village's standing as a "Tree City U.S.A.," which it has been since 1994. Trees are very important to village residents, and the village holds an annual Arbor Day celebration each year.

Orleans County

Orleans County was organized in 1824 from Genesee County and is named for the French Royal House of Orleans.

The Orleans County Courthouse was constructed in 1858 by William Barlow and may be regarded as his chief work. It serves as the focal point of the historic district, which is listed on the National Register of Historic Places. A number of the buildings in the historic district, including the county courthouse, use locally quarried Medina sandstone.

While the county seal shows an illustration of the large dome of the county courthouse, it has a strong canal presence today. Orleans County has twenty-six Erie Canal bridges and 40% of the lift bridges on the canal. Most date between 1909 and 1914 and represent a large infrastructure development. Although the bridges are owned by the state's Department of Transportation, their condition and maintenance easily affects the county.

Town of Ridgeway

Ridgeway is the largest town in Orleans County. The Town of Ridgeway was formed on June 8, 1812, and included what is now the towns of Barre, Carlton, Gaines, Shelby, and Yates.

The name derives from the Ridge Road which runs through Orleans County. The Town of Ridgeway is located in the western central part of Orleans County and is 8-1/4 miles across from east to west and 6 miles across from north to south. The northern half of the village of Medina is located in this town. There are three hamlets: Ridgeway, Knowlesville, and Oak Orchard On-the-Ridge.

Ridgeway has the only tunnel under the Erie Canal. It is illustrated on the seal along with an outline of an apple.

Village of Medina

Medina is a village in rural Orleans County on the Lake Ontario plains between Rochester and Buffalo, and is obscure even to many western New Yorkers.

Located east of the Village of Medina is a culvert, or tunnel, that allows you to drive under the Erie Canal, the only such place on the entire length of the canal. It was first built in 1823, and rebuilt at least twice, when the canal was widened and deepened there in 1854 and 1913.

Medina sandstone was discovered when the Erie Canal was dug through the area in 1824. It was prized for its quality and is found in many significant architectural buildings, such as the "Million Dollar Staircase" at the state capitol building in Albany. Three-quarters of the stone residential and public buildings in Buffalo use Medina sandstone. It can also be found in the Brooklyn Bridge and Buckingham Palace. Undoubtedly it was all shipped on the Erie Canal.

Although the village seal does not include the canal, the logo used here illustrates a packet boat being pulled by mules.

Town of Kendall

The Town of Kendall was named in honor of Amos Kendall, the United States Postmaster General at the time the township was formed on April 7, 1837.

The Erie Canal opened in 1825 making a ready market for wheat and lumber. It also made the way easier for more settlement. A group of 52 Norwegians came from Stavanger, Norway and made the first Norwegian settlement in modern America. They settled in a body along the shore of Lake Ontario in the northeast part of town. Eventually, the majority of them followed their leader, Cleng Peerson, to Illinois for what they perceived at the time as greener pastures. A few families remained here and there are reminders of their presence in Kendall to this day.

The seal illustrates a prosperous farm due to ready access to the canal for agricultural products.

Village of Holley

Located at the southern portion of Orleans County, the location was first settled by Augustus Southworth in 1820, where he served as an Assistant Engineer for construction on the Erie Canal. The Village of Holley was named in honor of Myron Holley, one of the first canal commissioners. The village was incorporated on September 3, 1850.

The seal illustrates man-made Holley Falls, which carries the overflow from the Erie Canal into Sandy Creek, a unique resource within the Erie Canalway National Heritage Corridor.

Village of Brockport

Settlement in Brockport began after a road was cut through the wilderness from Leroy in 1802. Brockport became a village around 1820, when the Erie Canal was laid out, and was incorporated on April 26, 1829. A note in the *Rochester Telegraph* of November 19, 1822 stated, "A village, called Brockport, is now erecting on the place where the Grand Canal intersects the main road leading from Clarkson to Leroy." It grew rapidly after the canal reached it, and industries developed to use the new waterway.

Hiel Brockway, a Connecticut-born builder, moved to the Town of Sweden in 1817. The name Brockport was said to be a shortened form of "Brockway's Port" and was selected in November of 1822.

Mary Ann Thorp designed the logo of the Village of Brockport around 1995 when she was mayor. It represents the bridges over the Erie Canal in the village.

Town of Ogden

Pioneers settled in the areas of Spencerport and Ogden as early as 1802. Early settlement took place in and around Ogden Center, a few miles south of Spencerport. However, once the Erie Canal arrived, commerce and settlement shifted to the Village area.

According to former Ogden Historian Earl White, the canal created a "new era of prosperity and growth" for Spencerport. Warehouses were built all along the canal and handled the sale and shipment of produce, such as cabbage, potatoes, tomatoes, cucumbers, watermelon, musk melon, pumpkins, apples, peaches, pears, and cherries from the fertile farms surrounding the village. As the years progressed, more people moved west and settled in the area.

Visitors walking, biking or boating along the canal often stop in Spencerport to refuel, have dinner, or pick up supplies. Small, unique shops and restaurants line Union Street and provide pleasant browsing and great eating for residents and visitors alike.

Village of Spencerport

Daniel Spencer's 180-acre farm, purchased in 1804, was later bisected by the canal during its construction. Spencer divided up the rest of his land into lots that were purchased by settlers. Thus, "Spencer's Basin" was firmly established as the business center of the Town of Ogden. But early in its development, residents decided that there were too many places along the canal with the word "Basin" in their names, and therefore changed the village name to "Spencerport."

In 1867, the New York State Legislature granted a petition to incorporate the village. The first election was held May 13, 1867.

The seals depicts a canal boat pulled by a mule, guided by his hoagie. The motto reveals the fact that with the days of canal transportation and commerce long past, the Spencerport of the 21st century is much more a residential community than a business hub.

City of Rochester

The Erie Canal was instrumental in the rapid growth and prosperity of the City of Rochester. During the canal days it was known as "The Flour City," but today as "The Flower City" for its annual Lilac Festival.

The Seal of the City of Rochester was designed by George Frauenberger and originally adopted by the Common Council on December 22, 1868. To the left of the shield, among other buildings, is depicted the dome of the old City Hall and a church spire. Below the buildings, a portion of the Erie Canal aqueduct spans the Genesee River. A canal boat loaded with flour barrels is being drawn by two mules. At the base below the shield is a flour barrel, a basket of apples, a plow, a water wheel, a cluster of grapes, a sheaf of grain, an anvil, a pumpkin, and other vegetables, all of which are bound with a scroll, upon which is the word "EXCELSIOR."

Village of Pittsford

Pittsford is a historic Erie Canal village, located seven miles southeast of Rochester in western New York. This small village has been remarkably successful in maintaining its distinctive small town character.

Pittsford is the oldest of Monroe County's ten incorporated villages. In 1814, the name Pittsford was adopted to honor the Vermont birthplace of Colonel Caleb Hopkins, a farmer, community leader and hero of the War of 1812.

Pittsford grew rapidly after the opening of the Erie Canal in 1822 and was incorporated as a village on July 4, 1827. Local entrepreneurs made fortunes from both canal construction and other businesses which benefited from the canal trade.

The seal illustrates a canal boat, a grain elevator (see page 78), and buildings within the town.

Town of Perinton

On April 6, 1813, the first town meeting was held in Cyrus Packard's tavern in Egypt, a thriving Perinton hamlet on the stagecoach road between Canandaigua and Rochester.

By the 1820s things were changing, as the Erie Canal opened up western New York. The Village of Fairport, an approximately one-square-mile area within the Town of Perinton, was drained of its unhealthy swamps by the new canal, and the north-south route through the village served as a natural highway for farmers to bring produce to the canal. The result was a booming canal town which eventually eclipsed the hamlet of Egypt as well as the surrounding canal settlements of Knapp's Bridge, Fullam's Basin, and Hartwell's (Bushnell's) Basin.

From the 1850s to the 1950s, Perinton's history was primarily Fairport's history. The village was not only an active canal port, but also developed into a booming industrial town.

Village of Fairport

Fairport was first settled in 1810 and grew with the success of the Erie Canal. It was not until 1822, three years before the completion of the Erie Canal, that Fairport really got started. With the canal open from Rochester to Little Falls, land was cleared and several farms started in and around the area. In 1827, the Fairport Hotel was built and in 1829 the Post Office was moved from Fullamtown to Fairport. The canal became an important transportation route and Fairport, with a hotel and a post office, became a popular stop for travelers. In fact, Fairport got its name from canal travelers who labeled the stop as a "pretty fair port." The name stuck. The village was incorporated in 1867.

   The people of Fairport recognize that its heritage as a small canal village is one of its biggest assets and they preserve it. Each June, Fairport's Canal Days Festival attracts more than 400 arts and crafts exhibitors from the U.S. and tens of thousands of visitors to one of the most anticipated festivals of its kind. The seal depicts a packet boat used for passenger travel on the canal.

Wayne County

The Erie Canal is a major attraction and recreational resource in Wayne County. It also had a huge impact on the villages of Macedon, Palmyra, Newark, Lyons, and Clyde. The canal provided inexpensive transport of goods which allowed agriculture and industry to develop. Local museums depict the canal era in many exhibits and remnants of the old canal are plentiful throughout the county. The canal takes center stage at numerous community events throughout the year. Wayne County has six locks, more than any other county.

The seal displays a recreational boat, and an apple is especially prominent. Wayne County is the third largest apple producing county in the nation.

Town of Macedon

The town was created in 1823. It is named after the birthplace of Alexander the Great.

The Erie Canal was an important factor in the settlement and growth of Macedon. Its two ports on the canal were Wayneport, formerly called West Macedon, and the village of Macedon itself.

The Wayneport Union Burying Ground, just north of the canal, is the final resting place of twenty-six "canallers," victims of an epidemic in 1846 during the construction of the Enlarged Canal. It is the only known mass burial site for canal laborers. The actual grave site is unmarked, but a historic marker erected in 1992 now identifies the location.

The Mud Creek Aqueduct is featured on the town seal and can be seen at Aqueduct Park at Lock 29.

Village of Macedon

The Village of Macedon is located in Wayne County in central New York and was incorporated in 1856. The village was home to many mills and tanneries, as well as Bickford & Huffman, the pioneer builders of fertilizer grain drills in America.

The Erie Canal was an important factor in the settlement and growth of Macedon. The village was known as the "Two Lock Town" because Locks 60 and 61 of the Enlarged Canal were located there. Today, Canal Park is located just off Route 350 in the village. The park includes the old Lock 61 (or Upper Macedon Lock), which is currently used as a spillway for Lock 30, a working lock of the Barge Canal System. Remains of Lock 60 or (Lower Macedon Lock) can also be seen along the Canal Trail.

Town of Palmyra

Although the Erie Canal was not completed until 1825, a substantial part was available for use by Palmyra by the middle of 1822.

The Palmyra area prospered tremendously in the canal period (1822-1853). Many of the Main Street commercial buildings were constructed between 1822 and 1830. Among the many occupations were farming (fruits, vegetables, grain, essence), manufacturing (boats, rope, lumber, ashes), and freight-forwarding.

The Town of Palmyra, originally called "Swift's Landing" after its founder General John Swift, was created in 1789. The town was also known as "District of Tolland" before adopting its present name in 1796. The Village of Palmyra, within the town, was incorporated in 1827.

Palmyra also has the distinction of being the birthplace of the Mormon religion and celebrates with the annual presentation of the Hill Cumorah Pageant.

The seal reflects a nautical heritage and the motto "Queen of Canal Towns."

Town of Arcadia

The Town of Arcadia was formed from the Town of Lyons on February 15, 1825.

The settlement of Newark was first called "Miller's Basin" in honor of Captain Joseph Miller, who contracted to build a section of the Erie Canal through this region. Around 1805 a new settlement began about three quarters of a mile east of Newark. It later became known as "Lockville" because of the three locks built near the settlement on the original Erie Canal. In 1839, the settlement of Lockville became incorporated as the Village of Arcadia. Newark and Lockville/Arcadia both prospered as a result of the canal, and in 1853, the Village of Newark was incorporated, including the former Village of Arcadia (Lockville) in the corporation.

The seal illustrates a bridge over the canal, a modern recreational boat, bountiful farms and produce, and a rose for the Jackson & Perkins Company, the famous rose growers that started in Newark.

Town of Lyons

The first settlers of European heritage, the Featherly and Stansell families, came to the area in 1789. In 1796, Charles Williamson gave the settlement the name of Lyons because the topography was similar to Lyon, France. The town was set off on March 1, 1811.

The Erie Canal provided an impetus for business and agriculture. Cheap transportation assured products could be shipped around the world. The enlarged Erie Canal and Barge canals continued to provide transportation for products to and from Lyons until the late-1800s. The Erie Canal continues to be developed for tourism and recreational purposes.

Among the industries that have come and gone, one deserves special mention. Peppermint was the cash crop for many farmers in the mid-1800s. The Hotchkiss Essential Oil Company became synonymous with the distillation of peppermint oil and continued until 1990. Lyons remembers this with a sprig of peppermint on their seal and the "Peppermint Days" festival each July.

Village of Clyde

Settlement of the area began in 1811 on the south bank of the Clyde River. Jonathan Melvin Jr. erected a house of hewn logs and it was there the first town meeting of Galen was held in 1812.

The river was named by Andrew McNab because it reminded him of the Clyde River in Scotland. He also christened the main street as Glasgow Street.

The Village of Clyde has its roots as an Erie Canal town, for the canal provided the initial means for industry to become the driving force behind the village's early growth. Many of these industries set Clyde apart from other small upstate New York communities. A unique glass works factory and a manufacturer who developed the first typewriter are only a few of Clyde's early industrial gems.

The Clyde River was canalized during the later canal enlargements. The seal reflects the town and a packet boat on the canal as seen through an arched window.

Town of Montezuma

The Town of Montezuma is located at the great bend in the Seneca River in Cayuga County. It is believed that Montezuma was named for the Aztec chieftain. The new seal depicts a packet boat.

Montezuma became the western terminus when the first section of the Erie Canal opened in 1820. Work on the "middle section" of the canal between Utica and Montezuma began after breaking ground in Rome in 1817. The Cayuga-Seneca Canal connected here to the Erie Canal in 1828, opening up 80 miles of navigation to the two largest Finger Lakes (see page 70).

The old seal illustrated the second longest aqueduct on the Enlarged Erie Canal of 1849, carrying canal waters over the Seneca River. It spanned 894 feet, with 31 magnificent arches. Today, the impressive remains of the Richmond Aqueduct are on the east side of the Seneca River, located in the Montezuma Heritage Park. The park also features several walking and nature trails with the historic remains of the three canals, locks, a dry dock and a paper mill.

Village of Port Byron

Port Byron is a village located about twenty-five miles west of Syracuse on Route 31 and seven miles north of Auburn on Route 38. The village sits at the center of the Town of Mentz.

Port Byron was a village on the Erie Canal and canal remains can be found in and around the village and town. East of the village, the enlarged canal can be seen at Schasel Park. There you will find a towpath walking trail that runs between Port Byron and Weedsport. It is a part of the New York State Canalway Trail, the cross-state recreational trail. To the west, the old canal can be followed as it passes through the muck lands, a place where onions and potatoes have been grown for generations. Port Byron was one of the very few villages where the route of the canal was changed during the enlargement of the canal in the 1850s. As such, vestiges of both canals can be found inside the village.

A primitive-style drawing of a canal boat was used for the Bicentennial seal in 1976.

Village of Weedsport

The Weed family of Auburn constructed a canal basin in the present village of Weedsport. This resulted in a shift of the population center from Macedonia (3/4 of a mile south) toward the center of the present village of Weedsport. The basin was used as a turning and docking area and repair facility for canal boats. The locality was first known as Weed's Basin, later as Weed's Port, and finally became Weedsport.

This seal is from Weedsport's Sesquicentennial in 1981 and shows an illustration of a canal boat and a mule on the upper half, and on the lower half, a scow going through a lock. Around the circumference are the other municipalities nearby including Macedonia, Brutus, and the original name of Weed's Basin. This seal is similar to one adopted in 1976 on the nation's bicentennial.

Village of Jordan

Jordan became a principal commercial, industrial and transportation center of western Onondaga County after one of the earliest sections of the Erie Canal was constructed through the village in 1819.

Jordan experienced a second economic spurt due to improvements made on the Jordan feeder canal and the advent of railroads. The originally small and narrow feeder had been enlarged in 1860. Between 1865 and 1885 the old canal was eliminated, the canal bed straightened, a new double lock constructed west of the village, and a larger aqueduct over Skaneateles Creek was built.

Jordan's unique display of 19th and early-20th century architecture illustrates its growth and prosperity through historically and architecturally significant residential, commercial, and ecclesiastical structures. A W.P.A. project in 1930 brought the canal new significance as a landscaped park and today is a visual tool for understanding canal and aqueduct construction. Various architectural styles, detailing, and methods of construction can be seen there.

Town of Elbridge

The town was first settled in 1793, when Josiah Buck and Captain William Stevens, a soldier of the Revolution, arrived in what is now the Town of Elbridge.

The Town of Elbridge was established in the year 1829. According to legend, the town was named after Elbridge Gerry. He was a member of the Boston Tea Party, a Signer of the Declaration of Independence and the Vice President of the United States from 1813-1814.

The town includes two incorporated villages: the Village of Jordan, an Erie Canal village and former center of trade and manufacturing; and the Village of Elbridge. The Village of Jordan became a major transportation center after one of the earliest sections of the Barge Canal was constructed through the village in 1819.

The Seal of the Town of Elbridge is a simple illustration of a canal boat.

Village of Liverpool

In 1797, a village was laid out by Simeon DeWitt (see page 73), at which time it was officially named Liverpool, though it had previously been known as "Little Ireland." Most of the inhabitants of the nine log cabins which constituted the village were Irish in origin. It was officially incorporated in 1830.

During the first decade of the nineteenth century, many new settlers arrived; they devoted themselves to making Liverpool a better place to live. Streets were laid out and named, trading areas were established.

In 1822 the outlet to the lake was changed as part of the Erie Canal project. The boom years for Liverpool began with the opening of the Erie Canal in 1825 and the Oswego Canal in 1828. When the Oswego Canal closed in 1918, the canal way of life ended. Salt duties provided for over half the cost for the canal system.

The new seal above, with the barrel of salt, reflects the history of making salt and was adopted around 2000.

City of Syracuse

What would one day be Syracuse was named Corinth in 1817. The City of Syracuse was incorporated in 1848, and soon after its Market Hall Building was renamed City Hall.

Syracuse's low, swampy land was ideal for canal construction. The Erie Canal opened in 1825 and quickly established Syracuse's dominance over nearby settlements, including the Village of Salina. As a result of the boom of the early canal years, the villages of Salina and Syracuse merged to become the City of Syracuse. Syracuse's nickname is the "Salt City." Some people say that Syracuse was the city that salt built. But in reality, the city was built because of the Erie Canal, which continued to run through the heart of the city until the mid-1920s.

The city seal features four illustrative elements: the Erie Canal, the salt-blocks, the railroads, and the factories.

Village of Chittenango

The Village of Chittenango was incorporated in 1842. *Chittenango* is an Indian word meaning "where the waters run north." Gypsum was discovered in the hills near Chittenango. John B. Yates built a plaster mill and manufactured water lime or hydraulic cement (see pages 73 and 79), which was used in building the Erie Canal. The Erie Canal reached this area in 1820 and by that time a lateral canal was planned and built to the middle of the village. The Enlarged Canal with its dry dock opened about 1855 and helped the village to prosper.

    Chittenango was the home of Frank Baum who wrote The Wizard of Oz. His characters and the rainbow along with yellow brick road are included on the seal. The seal also illustrates a canal boat with a mule on the towpath, and the abundant wildlife in the area. Chittenango Falls, in the top center, drops 167 feet down a nearly-even cascade of Onondaga Limestone stairs. The formal building with columns was used as the Chittenango Bank, the First National Bank of Chittenango, the post office (1913) and finally as a library.

Village of Canastota

Canastota is an Indian word meaning "three pines." The village is an Erie Canal community central to a region rich in historical tradition.

Originally settled in 1810, Canastota evolved into a vibrant canal town and became incorporated in 1835. A revitalized portion of the canal still exists, running through the central portion of the village. The Canal Town Museum is located just across the street from the canal. Many homes from the canal period still exist throughout the village. Products manufactured in Canastota, such as Canastota Cut Glass and Sherwood sleds and wagons, are highly valued in the antiques market.

Canastota is also home to the International Boxing Hall of Fame which honors local Carmen Basilio, "the upstate onion farmer."

The seal includes a canal boat, a tractor signifying the importance of agriculture to the village, a locomotive for transportation and onions and potatoes from the local mucklands, recognized country-wide.

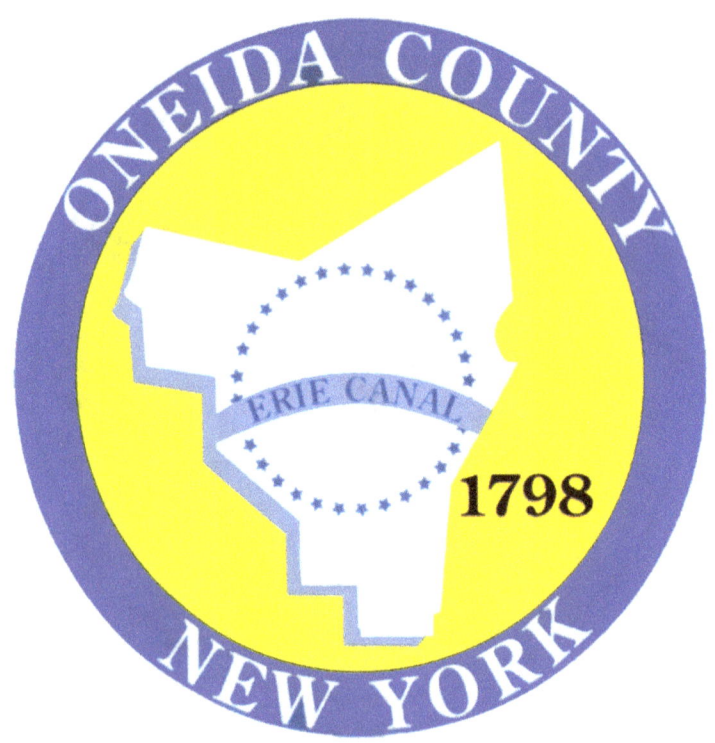

Oneida County

When the canal was completed in 1825, it became an immediate success. Revenues poured in as 218,000 tons of freight were carried the first year. The cost of shipping a ton of cargo from Albany to Buffalo dropped from $120 to less than $8. The value of land along the canal increased greatly. On October 22, 1819, the first 96-mile section between Rome and Utica was opened as a political maneuver by Governor Clinton to secure further funding. The canal boat that traveled down the section was named *Chief Engineer*, in honor of Benjamin Wright who was the Engineer for the "Middle Section." Both Rome and Utica are in Oneida County.

The success of the Erie prompted the building of two lateral canals in Oneida County, the Chenango and the Black River Canals, begun in 1836. (See page 70)

The seal is an outline of the county with a band that shows that the Erie Canal stretches from border to border.

Village of Sylvan Beach

Although the community was founded in 1840, it was not incorporated until 1971. It has been a resort and tourist destination since the 1880s.

The original Erie Canal bypassed Oneida Lake but the enlarged Erie Barge Canal built beginning in 1916 used the lake as part of the canal system.

A 4.5 ton buoy (#106) that bobbed near the entrance of the Erie Canal into Oneida Lake was eventually taken out of service and given a prominent spot in the village park, next to the Sylvan Beach Amusement Park.

The buoy is at least fifty years old and originally had an oil lamp. Canal crews had to light it every night. Later, it was converted to battery power. Today, the red light atop the buoy is powered by electricity.

The buoy has become the new village logo and is one of the more unusual ones in the state.

Town of Verona

A part of the Town of Westmoreland, the hamlet of Verona was then known as Hand's Village, named for Captain Ichabod Hand, who had a public house there. No one seems to know how or when the village became known as "Verona." The Town of Verona was formally established on February 17, 1802. The illustration is on the town flag, which shows a typical canal boat.

The Erie Canal dissects the town. Many small communities grew up along its banks, among them Durhamville, State Bridge, Dunbarton, Stark's Landing, Verona Landing, Higginsville, Stacy Basin, Grove Springs, and New London. It was in these places that the canallers found general stores, hotels, blacksmith shops, dry docks, and other facilities to accommodate their life-style.

City of Rome

On July 4, 1817, the ground was first broken for the Erie Canal. The Hon. Joshua Hathaway cast the first shovel-full of dirt. Thousands of spectators were present and cannons were fired in celebration. At the end of 1817, only fifteen miles had been completed. At that rate the canal would have taken over 30 years to complete, but the canal from Montezuma to Utica was so far completed as to be navigable in 1820. The Erie Canal, as first constructed, passed a half mile south of the village, but when it was enlarged its channel was made through the village.

The success of the canal led to most other canals and later some railroads being started on the 4th of July.

The seal depicts Fort Stanwix, which was built in 1758, by Brig. Gen. John Stanwix. Fort Stanwix was important during the American Revolution.

Village of Whitesboro

The village was founded by pioneer Hugh White after the American Revolution. He was highly regarded by his neighbors and by the Oneida Indians who would hold games at his property. At one such gathering a local chief defeated all challengers at wrestling and he then challenged Hugh White himself. As the story goes, he was conflicted between accepting and losing or declining and fearing ridicule. He accepted, and the chief stepped into a pothole, fell over backward and Hugh White landed on top of him and won the match. This further cemented good relations between Hugh White and the Oneidas. The seal depicting the event has been the subject of much controversy over the past few years.

Two of Hugh White's grandsons, Canvass White (see page 73) and Hugh White III, were instrumental in developing the Erie Canal and essentially eliminated the frontier along the Mohawk River and Central New York. Hugh's 1830 house in Waterford is now the historical museum (see page 91).

City of Utica

Utica was settled in 1773 on the site of the abandoned Fort Schuyler. The name is reported to have been picked out of a hat, and is named after Utica, Tunisia. Utica was incorporated as a village on April 3, 1798. It was formed as a town April 7, 1817, and was incorporated as a city, February 13, 1832. The Erie Canal stimulated the city's economic growth when, two years after the canal was begun in Rome on October 22, 1819, the section between Utica and Rome was opened. Thousands cheered as the first boat to travel on the Erie Canal, the 60-foot *Chief Engineer*, named for Benjamin Wright of Rome (see page 75), left Rome for Utica towed by one horse.

The seal of Utica reflects an earlier time in Utica's history and honors the Onondaga Indians whose ancestral home covered this part of the country.

Village of Frankfort

Frankfort was incorporated in 1863. An early settler was Lawrence Frank, for whom the town was named. Early pioneers were German immigrants, who were called "Palatines" because they came from the Lower Palatinate of the Rhine River. They settled in the Mohawk Valley prior to the Revolutionary War, building mills on the river and creeks.

William Gates established the plant along the Erie Canal for the manufacturing of wooden matches. All work was done by hand until Mr. Gates invented machinery. He later added other buildings and by the 1850s the Match Factory was the largest employer in the town of Frankfort, employing over 300 workers. A paper company later took over the buildings and today there is a monument in the park commemorating the founding of the Match Factory.

The seal illustrated here was adopted for the village bicentennial.

Village of Ilion

The Village of Ilion is situated on the south bank of the Mohawk River in the town of German Flats. The town was first settled around 1725 by the German Palatines. With the completion of the Erie Canal in 1825 the village began to really flourish. On the canal list it was called "Steele's Creek," but it was also known as "Morgan's Landing," and there was an early settlement called "New London."

In 1828 Eliphalet Remington (1793-1861) established a small factory for the manufacture of rifles. From 1830 to 1843 the village was known as "Remington's Corners," and the first post office established in 1845 was named "Remington." The village was incorporated under the name of Ilion in 1852 as Remington was opposed to the use of his name for the village.

The seal is an illustration of a gunsmith, presumably Eliphalet Remington, holding a Remington rifle.

City of Little Falls

As a precursor to the historic Erie Canal, The Western Inland Lock Navigation Company was formed in 1792. It was George Washington who first recommended the building of a canal around the rapids at Little Falls, and under the leadership of his friend General Philip Schuyler, work was begun in 1793 and completed in 1795—thirty years before the completion of the Erie Canal (see page 76). The canal was in operation for less than twenty-five years. Although economically unsuccessful, it served to demonstrate the importance and possibilities of water transportation in the state.

The contemporary Erie Canal is a significant feature of the City of Little Falls. A week long annual Canal Celebration has been held since 1987.

The seal is a photograph of Lock 17 at Little Falls. The lock was once the highest in the world at 40-1/2 feet.

Town of St. Johnsville

Nathan Brown owned the Pilot Line Company. It was in his boat, *Seneca Chief*, and under his direction, that Governor DeWitt Clinton was conveyed from Buffalo to Albany to celebrate the opening of the Erie Canal. By 1830, Brown retired to his farm in the Town of Oppenheim.

    The canal was to mean much to St. Johnsville and its industry. In 1825 James Averell & Sons located here. They built a distillery and tannery on Zimmerman Creek and took advantage of the Erie Canal's shipping facilities. Manufacturers such as M. Williams established the St. Johnsville Agricultural Works, making various farming implements. Other principal products of St. Johnsville in the 1800s included castings, paper, carpets, and woolen goods. The area had fine stone quarries in the hills above town, which were used to supply stone used in the building of the Erie Canal. The canal paralleled the Mohawk River at St. Johnsville until 1842 when it was filled in and the railroad laid.

Village of Fultonville

Every community has its own unique history and the Village of Fultonville is no exception. Seated in the heart of Montgomery County on the south bank of the Mohawk River, this community's origins began much earlier than its date of incorporation.

In 1750, John Evart Van Epps purchased 900 acres of marshland in the area that became known as "Van Epps' Swamp." John Starin opened one of the first taverns around 1810. However, the construction of the Erie Canal catapulted the community's growth. By the time the waterway began operations in 1825, area officials had the streets laid out, and a variety of businesses opened their doors, including a flour mill, distillery, mercantile, saw mill, blacksmith shop, and potashery. Along Main Street was a flurry of activity with the construction of homes, most of which were built by Maynard Starin and Thomas Robinson. The canal's enlargement there in the 1830s brought more businesses to this prospering community.

On August 9, 1848, the community, now known as Fultonville, in honor of steamboat inventor Robert Fulton, incorporated as a village.

Life in Fultonville thrived, as this was a major transportation center exporting freight, specifically lumber, from the Adirondacks, as well as from Fonda, Johnstown, and Gloversville. A variety of manufacturers continued operations in Fultonville for a long time, including a furniture company, Wemple & Yates Foundry, a broom-making company, and a manufacturer from Vermont that eased the burdens of some homemakers. White Mop Wringer began producing wooden mop wringers in 1893, turning to production of the steel-fashioned wringers by the 1920s.

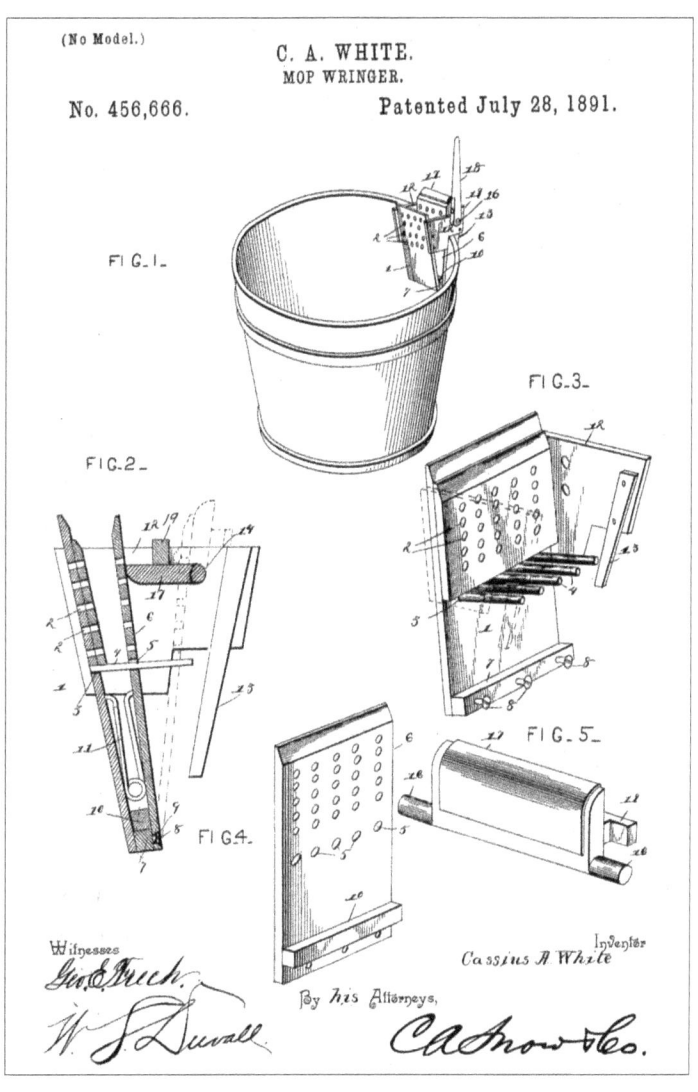

City of Amsterdam

The Mohawk Turnpike, the Erie Canal, and the railroads all came in rapid succession after 1800. The steep drop to the river that had hindered early development now propelled it with the force of a creek that drops 300 feet in its last three miles. By 1832, the hamlet incorporated as a village; by 1885, the city was chartered.

The manufacturers of linseed oil, brooms, knit ware, buttons, iron goods, and above all—carpets—were located here, including two of the world's most recognized brand names, Sanford-Bigelow and Mohawk.

An earlier seal (c. 1900) promoted Amsterdam's industrialization. The seal reflected the manufacture of most of the items listed above, surrounded by buttons. Many immigrant families supplemented their income by sewing buttons on cards at home and turning them into the factories, getting paid as piecework. The seal was eventually replaced by the illustration of a Dutch windmill, shown above.

Schenectady County

The illustrations around the seal on the Schenectady County flag includes a Schenectady boat and a sheaf of broom corn. The area had one of the first canal systems in the country, with the Western Inland Lock Navigation Company, promoted by Gen. Philip Schuyler (see page 76). It led the way for Schenectady to become a famous boat-building community, making *bateaux* (flat bottom boats), "Durham Boats" (a larger, double-pointed *bateau*), and a large cargo boat known as the "Schenectady Boat." Schenectady County, in particular the City of Schenectady, the Village of Scotia and the Town of Glenville, was famous for making brooms during the 19th century. The county's broom corn industry began about 1812, and reached its peak between 1840 and 1860. Broom corn dominated the Mohawk River flats, and a number of factories strove to meet the wide demand for the product. At one point, the city was the center of the industry in the U.S., making a million brooms a year.

Town of Rotterdam

The area that is now the town of Rotterdam, New York was first settled predominately by the Dutch, about the year 1661. The town, named after the city of Rotterdam, The Netherlands, was formed from a ward of the city of Schenectady on April 14, 1820.

The fertile soil along the Mohawk River was responsible for a thriving broom corn industry during the mid-1800s. With the advent of the Erie Canal in 1825 and later, with the coming of railroads to Rotterdam, hamlets began to spring up, including Rotterdam. The Erie Canal traversed the entire length of northeast Rotterdam, with two locks located in the town. Athens Junction and Mohawkville were quiet, pleasant settlements in the southeastern part of town.

Established as a first class town in 1942, Rotterdam has since adopted the seal of the Old World Rotterdam, along with its motto, translated as "Stronger Through Effort."

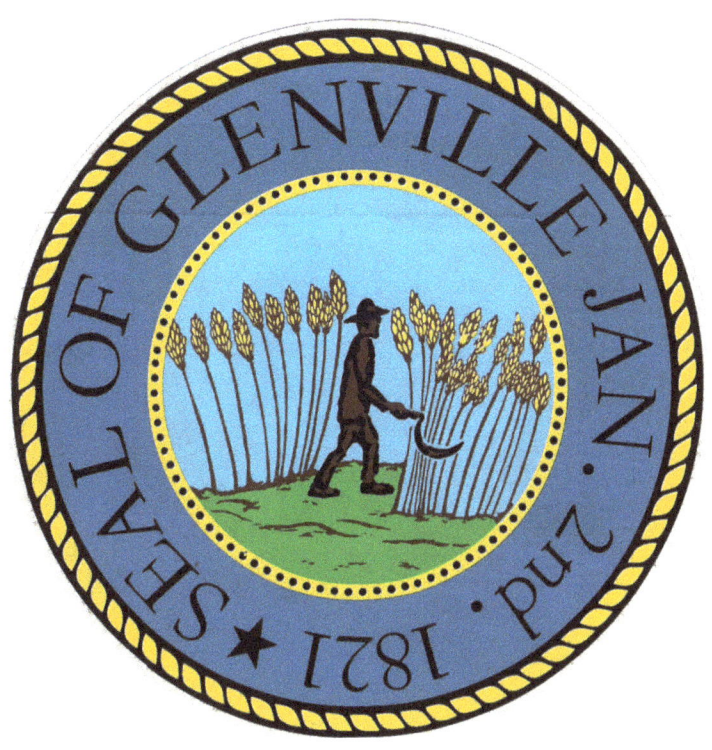

Town of Glenville

Glenville, named in honor of Alexander Lindsey Glen, a native of Scotland and the patentee of the township, was formed from Schenectady, April 14, 1820. The Mohawk Flats are very fertile and were devoted to a great extent to raising broom corn.

The Village of Scotia was formed within the town in 1904. In the mid-1800s Scotia was well known as the center of the broom industry with almost 100 operating broom corn farms, manufacturing up to 1,000,000 brooms a year. Eventually, broom corn from the West was more competitive and the industry declined.

The seal illustrates a farmer harvesting broom corn.

City of Schenectady

Schenectady was first settled in 1661 when the area was part of the Dutch colony of New Netherlands. Settlement was led by Arent Van Curler of Nijkerk in the Netherlands, who was granted letters of patent in 1684, but who owned a plot there since 1661. It was chartered as a borough in 1765, and incorporated as a city March 26, 1798. It is also the home of Union College, chartered by the New York State Regents in 1795.

Schenectady became the point of embarkation for passengers going west on the Erie Canal. Eventually the Erie Canal was filled in and became Erie Boulevard. Even today many of the local businesses display murals or photographs of the canal on their walls.

The shock of wheat is prominent on the seal of the City of Schenectady, recalling the "fair land" of the Mohawk Valley and symbolizing peace and plenty. Wheat was farmed extensively prior to broom corn in the 1800s and was the source of wealth at an earlier time.

Town of Niskayuna

The Town of Niskayuna was formed on March 6, 1809. As of 1822, the Erie Canal crossed the river into Niskayuna from Rexford on an aqueduct 748 feet long and 25 feet above the water. Known as the Rexford Aqueduct, a major portion was removed in 1918 when the new State Barge Canal System was built. The remnants of the southern side of the Rexford Aqueduct are in Niskayuna. Erie Canal's Lock 7 Park in Niskayuna has picnic facilities and is a place to watch boats go through the lock.

The Niskayuna Bicentennial Town Seal was designed by area resident Robert Banks and was adopted in 1976. The upper right side depicts an Indian holding an ear of corn. The five tepees in the background represent the Five Nations. The name *Niskayuna* means "land of extended corn fields." The lower right portrays a Shaker farmer; upper left pictures an Erie Canal boat in tow; and lower left is the atomic symbol, for modern industry in Niskayuna. In the center is a map of the town with typical crops below the stonework letter "N".

Town of Clifton Park

The Town of Clifton Park developed primarily as a result of transportation patterns. The first settlements at Fort's Ferry, Vischer Ferry, and Rexford Flats were along the river, which was the chief means of transportation. Ferries established at these points became the focus for village life. Roads and turnpikes developed across the town from paths and Indian trails. Taverns and villages grew up along the roads to serve independent travelers and stagecoach traffic.

    The Erie Canal would give added life and population to Vischer Ferry and Rexford. The heyday of the canal was the "boom town" era of these two hamlets. Never again would they support such industry and activity.

    The bottom section of the shield includes the rolling land of Clifton Park along the Mohawk River. The stylized portrayal of water is representative of the Mohawk River and the Erie Canal's transportation and agricultural importance to the growth and development of Clifton Park.

City of Cohoes

Of the original 83 locks on the Erie Canal, 19 were in Cohoes to surmount the Cohoes Falls. Even when the Erie Canal was enlarged beginning in 1836, Cohoes had 10 of the 72 lift locks. When the Barge Canal was completed in 1916 by utilizing the Mohawk and Hudson Rivers, Cohoes and the "Albany Cut" that went through Watervliet and Menands to Albany was bypassed altogether by the locks in Waterford.

The "industrial founder" of Cohoes was Canvass White, one of the original canal engineers (see page 73). Cohoes had abundant water power for industry and many knitting mills developed there. The canals and the Hudson River made it easy to get raw material into Cohoes and finished goods out, so mills were very profitable. Since lodging and taverns were needed for the boatmen and stables for the animals, Cohoes grew rapidly and was incorporated by 1869. Along with industrial products, the seal illustrates Harmony Mills Number Three. Completed in 1872, it was the largest individual cotton mill in the world.

The Great Cohoes Falls

Cohoes is derived from an Indian name meaning "place of the falling canoe." It is the second largest falls in the state after Niagara and is the reason that Little Falls was designated as such to differentiate it from Cohoes.

Not much press even locally is given to the Cohoes Falls but it was a huge obstacle to completing the Erie Canal and a source of power prior to electricity. Of the original 83 locks, 27 were needed to get from the Hudson River to Schenectady. Even today the Waterford Flight of Locks 2 through 6 is required to overcome the drop of over 70 feet of the Cohoes Falls.

Today there is an observation area and stairs leading to the base of the falls. Hydroelectric power is still generated at the falls. *(Photo courtesy of Richard Vang.)*

Town of Waterford

The Town of Waterford is situated at the junction of the Hudson and Mohawk Rivers, and the junction of the Erie and Champlain Canals. It is the home of the "Waterford Flight," the highest set of lift locks in the world. The seal shows Lock 2.

In 1816 the old precinct of *Halve Maan* (Halfmoon) was divided into two separate towns, Halfmoon and Waterford. The Village of Waterford is located in the town and is the oldest continuously incorporated village in the nation.

The Champlain Canal opened on September 10, 1823. Construction of the Waterford Flight in 1915 as part of the Barge Canal System assured Waterford's role in canal transport through the twentieth century. Waterford became a major gateway to the canal system which provided a route west to Buffalo and the Great Lakes and north to Whitehall, Lake Champlain, and Canada. With the presence of water for both power and transportation, the Hudson-Mohawk region became one of the birthplaces of the American Industrial Revolution.

The Waterford waterfront annually plays host to hundreds of boaters exploring the canals and rivers, as well as canal and tugboat festivals.

City of Troy

The Troy Federal Lock is located in the City of Troy on the Hudson River three miles south of the Erie Canal and Champlain Canal junction at Waterford. It was opened in 1916 and was one of the first modern locks along the present-day canal system.

    Although not a part of the Erie Canal, it is the first lock that a boater would approach when traveling northbound on the Hudson River. It is located 134 nautical miles north of the Battery in Manhattan and marks the end of federal waters.

    This lock once stood as Lock 1 of the Erie Canal, but was later transferred to the U.S. Government and is still operated by the Army Corps of Engineers.

    The seal of the City of Troy shows Dutch sloops on the Hudson that were the principal means of shipping prior to bridges, railroads, and the Erie Canal.

Rensselaer Polytechnic Institute

In March of 1810, a commission was chosen by the New York State Legislature, consisting of seven persons—Gouverneur Morris, DeWitt Clinton, and Stephen Van Rensselaer among the more important—for the purpose of exploring a route for a proposed western canal. Van Rensselaer ultimately spent nearly twenty-nine years as a canal commissioner. The Erie Canal was essentially built without formal engineering training and has been called America's first "school" of engineering. Stephan Van Rensselaer saw the need for trained engineers and in 1824 co-founded, with Amos Eaton, what became Rensselaer Polytechnic Institute (see pages 74 and 75).

The R.P.I. seal has evolved over the years into a new form. The seal illustrated here is an older design. It was created in the early 1900s, incorporating the institute's coat-of-arms, which in turn was based on the Van Rensselaer family coat-of-arms.

City of Watervliet

Today Watervliet is not known for the Erie Canal, but it played a huge role in the past. The boatmen and canallers often received their pay in Watervliet and had to wait for their boats to return from New York City for another trip west for more goods. Dozens of taverns catered to the hard-drinking, hard-working boatmen, who were mostly Irish that found work on the boats after the canal was completed. It became known as a rowdy town and street brawls were common.

During the peak of the canal period in Watervliet, it handled more tonnage than any other port on the canal or Hudson River except New York City. The canal ran behind the current Watervliet Arsenal and through Schuyler Flatts Cultural Park. A historical marker and large stones that outline the location of the canal can be found there.

The seal the sun rising over the hills east of the Hudson, a sheaf of wheat and a cornucopia to signify bounty, the steamship *Clermont* and a Dutch sloop.

Village of Menands

This area, situated along the river flats north of Albany, was mostly agricultural farm land where people raised wheat and various livestock. The Hudson River, Erie Canal (1825), and Watervliet Turnpike (1830) were the principal means of transportation north and south along the river.

Menands was incorporated on August 15th, 1924. The area was called "Menands" or "Menands Garden" because of the well known horticulturist and gardener, Louis Menand. He owned a flower shop where Albany residents bought flowers to put on the graves in Albany Rural Cemetery nearly across the street. It came to be known as "Menand's Flower shop" or simply as Menands.

The village seal was designed for its 50th Anniversary in 1974. The seal has a bust of Louis Menand in the center. To the left are a stand of trees signifying wilderness and to the right the Delaware & Hudson Railroad and below, a mule tender on the Erie Canal.

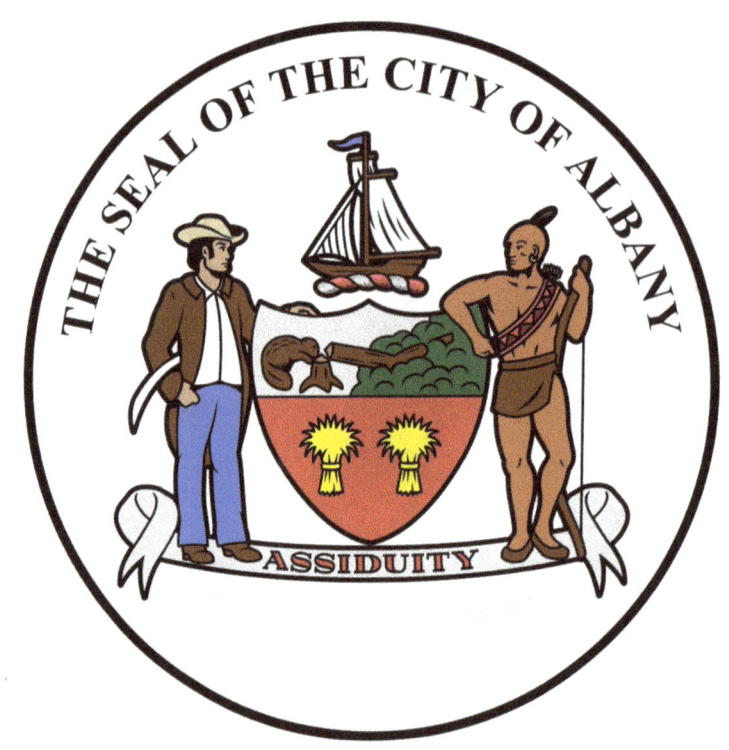

City of Albany

The original terminus of the Erie Canal was at Albany. Along with two bridges and a pier, the "Albany Basin" enclosed roughly 32 acres of the Hudson River. It could accommodate 1,000 canal boats and 50 steamboat moorings. From there the canal boats were tied together and traveled to New York City. Later the enlarged canal system moved the terminus to Waterford.

The seal of Albany represents an earlier time in the city's history, when they were settled by the Dutch. It was designed by Simon DeWitt, who served on Washington's staff during the Revolution and became the Surveyor General of New York for 50 years.

The shield recognizes the two principal industries; fur trade and the manufacture of flour. The supporters of the shield represent a farmer of the colonial period and an American Indian. The crest, a Dutch sloop under sail, which underscores the importance of commerce. The motto, "ASSIDUITY" indicates the dominant virtue of its citizens—assiduous labor which "conquers all."

New York City

Prior to the Erie Canal, New Orleans stood to gain from goods shipped on the Mississippi River. In addition, goods shipped by way of the Saint Lawrence River would have benefited Canada more than the young United States. At that time, New York City was fifth in size among the nation's ports. Boston, Philadelphia, New Orleans, Charleston, and Baltimore were all larger.

Because of the canal, goods instead were diverted through New York City. After the Erie Canal opened, New York City became the largest port and has never relinquished the title.

The success of the Erie Canal also led to the nickname for New York as "The Empire State" because of the effect it had on the state and the nation. It grew more wealthy than many European empires.

The seal of the city is similar to that of Albany, illustrating a Dutch heritage, including a windmill.

Appendix 1:
Other Canals in New York State

The Erie Canal was so successful that every other state began building canals to compete. New York State also began to build more canals—"lateral" or "feeder" canals—to take advantage of the Grand Canal. Many communities lobbied for a canal or a connection to the Erie.

Other canals that were constructed in New York include:

- Black River canal, from Rome to Carthage
- Cayuga & Seneca Canal, from Montezuma to Geneva
- Champlain Canal, from Waterford to Whitehall
- Chemung Canal, from Montour Falls to Elmira
- Crooked Lake Canal, from Dresden to Penn Yann
- Genesee Canal, from Rochester to Olean
- Oneida Lake Canal, from Higginsville to Sylvan Beach
- Oswego Canal, from Syracuse to Oswego.

But at the present day, the towns along these secondary canals and feeder canals have chosen other symbols to represent their heritage rather than symbols that represent canals. For example, the Champlain Canal overlays the earlier history of the Revolutionary War and the Battle of Saratoga, themes which are evident in several municipal seals.

One town that has included a canal boat and a mule is the Town of Big Flats in the Southern Tier of New York near the Pennsylvania border. The town was on the Feeder Canal which had been built from Gibson through Big Flats and joined the Chemung Canal at Horseheads, a sixteen-mile waterway. This opened in 1833, bringing an immense amount of traffic through Big Flats. By 1850, an estimated one-eighth of all tonnage of coal, grain and lumber to or from Albany passed through the feeder canal.

In Oneida County, the success of the Erie Canal prompted the building of two lateral canals. Both the Chenango and the Black River canals were begun in 1836. The Chenango Canal from Binghamton to Utica came at an opportune time for Utica. It was converting its textile mills to steam power and needed coal from Pennsylvania to produce that steam. The Black River began in Rome and proceeded north to the Black River in Carthage.

Unfortunately, the lateral canals proved to be of marginal value at best. Railroads, and later, modern highways combined to make these canals less important or obsolete. But some are still operational as part of the greater canal system and are open to traffic today.

Champlain Canal Lock C5 is just north of Schuylerville on the Hudson River. This lock is interesting as it is actually the site of two locks, the current Lock 5 and a junction lock that once connected the modern Champlain Canal and the former Champlain Canal which ran through the heart of Schuylerville. The junction lock no longer operates, but is worth a look if you are interested in the canal's history. *(Photo courtesy of Richard Vang.)*

Appendix 2:
Notable Men of the Erie Canal

Jessie Hawley (1773 - 1842)

Jessie Hawley was a flour merchant who was unable to ship his flour profitably by overland routes and who eventually went bankrupt and was put into debtors' prison. While there, he wrote several articles advocating for an inland canal route as early as 1805. They included economic projections based on the success of canals in Europe that eventually interested DeWitt Clinton. Upon completion of the Erie Canal in 1825, Clinton gave credit to Hawley for the concept of the Erie Canal. He accompanied Clinton on the inaugural trip from Buffalo to New York City. He later went on to become a well-respected treasurer of the Village of Lockport. *(Portrait artist unknown. Image source: https://www.findagrave.com.)*

DeWitt Clinton (1769 - 1828)

DeWitt Clinton was a politician who served in the New State Legislature, became a U.S. Senator, Mayor of New York City and Governor of New York State. As governor, he is generally credited with getting the Erie Canal built. The sheer scope of the project led many to believe it could not be accomplished and ridiculed it as "Clinton's Ditch." It required a champion to promote an unprecedented project over an extended period with tremendous costs and an uncertain outcome. But despite opposition, he persisted in his vision of the canal and proved equal to the task. He is rightly remembered as the "Father of the Erie Canal." *(Portrait by Rembrandt Peale. Image source: Wikimedia Commons.)*

Simeon DeWitt (1756 - 1834)

Simeon DeWitt became Surveyor General of New York State following the end of the Revolution. In 1810 he was appointed to the Erie Canal Commission to study the feasibility of the canal. The War of 1812 delayed plans for the canal. It was under his tenure that the towns in the Military Tract (some along the Erie Canal) were named with classical Greek and Roman names. *(Portrait by Ezra Ames. Image source: Wikimedia Commons.)*

Canvass White (1790 - 1834)

When the canal was begun in 1817, there were no trained engineers other than surveyors in the entire country. Canvass White traveled to England and walked over 200 miles to observe every canal in the country. He saw how the locks were built and took notes and made drawings. Upon his return, he invented hydraulic cement, which dries under water and was used extensively to build locks on the Erie Canal. In 1826, with the backing of DeWitt Clinton, Peter Remsen and Stephen Van Rensselaer, he became president of the Cohoes Company, formed to take advantage of water power from the Cohoes Falls. He is the only person who has both his first and last name used as street names in Cohoes. *(Engraved portrait by Charles B. Stuart. Image source: Wikimedia Commons.)*

James Geddes (1763 - 1838)

James Geddes was a judge, surveyor and self-trained engineer. He served in the New York State Assembly and met Simeon DeWitt, who persuaded him that a canal connecting the Hudson River and Lake Erie was feasible. Geddes surveyed a possible route in 1808. His route was very close to the one actually chose. Geddes was Assistant Chief Engineer for the Erie Canal and later served as Chief Engineer on the Champlain Canal. The Ohio Canal Commission also hired him to survey the canal routes that became the Ohio & Erie Canal and the Miami & Erie Canal. In addition, he surveyed canal routes in Pennsylvania and Maine.

Stephen Van Rensselaer III (1764 - 1839)

As an heir to the fortune of Killian Van Rensselaer ("The Patroon"), he was one of the wealthiest men in America. He served in the U.S. Congress and was a member of the New York State Canal Commission, beginning in 1816. He served as president of the commission from 1825 until his death in 1839. Through his planning and involvement with the Erie Canal, he recognized the need for trained engineers in the country and was a co-founder of Rensselaer Polytechnic Institute in 1824. The logo or seal of R.P.I. is a variation of the Van Rensselaer coat-of-arms (see page 65). *(Portrait by Gilbert Stuart. Image courtesy of National Gallery of Art.)*

Amos Eaton (1776 - 1842)

Amos Eaton was a scientist and an educator. As a scientist, he performed geological surveys of the Erie Canal. He co-founded Rensselaer Polytechnic Institute (see page 65) with financial backing from Stephen Van Rensselaer and was the first Senior Professor. *(Portrait artist unknown. Image source Wikimedia Commons.)*

Nathan Roberts (1776 - 1851)

The most difficult part of the Erie Canal was conquering the Niagara Escarpment, which was a 60-foot tall rock formation. It would take five locks in succession, but the time required for a boat to navigate all five before a boat could go in the opposite direction would have caused a significant bottleneck, so the design required a new approach. Several engineers submitted plans to accomplish the challenge and Nathan Robert's proposal was accepted. His double-lock "Flight of Five" in Lockport was considered an engineering marvel.

Benjamin Wright (1770 - 1842)

Benjamin Wright was appointed as Chief Engineer for the canal. Because of his success, he was later hired to engineer the Chesapeake & Ohio Canal and the Saint Lawrence Ship Canal. In 1969, the American Society of Civil Engineers (A.S.C.E.) declared him "The Father of American Civil Engineering." *(Portrait artist unknown. Image source: Wikimedia Commons.)*

John B. Jervis (1795 - 1885)

John Jervis was a superintendent on a fifty-mile section of Erie Canal. He later became Chief Engineer for the Delaware & Hudson Canal. He convinced the company to include a railroad in the project; he then designed the "Stourbridge Lion" locomotive, built in England but one of the first locomotives to run in the U.S. He also designed and supervised construction of the Chenango Canal and the Croton Aqueduct, which supplied water to New York City.

Philip Schuyler (1733 - 1804)

Philip Schuyler was a general in the Revolution. After seeing England's canal system in operation in 1760, he became a strong advocate for a proposed canal to connect the Hudson River to lakes Ontario and Champlain. In the N.Y.S. Legislature he proposed a bill to charter both the Western and the Northern Inland Lock Navigation companies. In 1792 he became the president of both companies. The Western constructed a series of dams, locks, and short canal segments along the Mohawk River and across the drainage divide at Rome, allowing *bateaux* and Durham boats to carry cargo from Schenectady to Oneida Lake, the Finger Lakes, and Lake Ontario two decades before the Erie Canal. Despite Schuyler's investments in the upper Hudson Valley, the Northern accomplished far less. The Champlain Canal would take another three decades.

George Washington (1732 - 1797)

Though not directly connected to the Erie Canal, George Washington was interested in canals even before becoming President. He knew that people would settle west of the Appalachians and feared their isolation from the thirteen coastal states unless they were connected through commerce. In 1785, he became president of the Potowmack Canal Company and honorary president of the James River Company, both chartered to construct canals across Virginia.

Appendix 3:
Inventions from the Erie Canal

As the Erie Canal was built, unforeseen obstacles had to be overcome. The term "Yankee ingenuity" came about during the building of the canal. Problems came up as work progressed and practical solutions were found by the people at the construction sites. New tools were invented because they were necessary. This spirit of inventiveness is one of many legacies from the Erie Canal.

Wheelbarrow

The Chinese invented the wheelbarrow and there is evidence of wheelbarrows in use by stonemasons in Europe during the Middle Ages, but in the early stages of the Erie Canal it had to be redesigned. Existing carts of the time were rectangular and had to be loaded and unloaded by the shovelful. Jeremiah Brainard designed the wheelbarrow with the familiar rounded sides and was granted a patent on August 26, 1819. The rounded sides, along with the single wheel, allowed the wheelbarrow to be dumped more easily and did not require a shovel to unload it. His design is the same basic wheelbarrow in use today.

Early wheelbarrow design. *(Image source: Wikimedia Commons.)*

Brainard's wheelbarrow design. *(Image source: Wikimedia Commons.)*

Grain Elevator

The production of grain in the Midwest overwhelmed the capacity of the Erie Canal. Large ships on the Great Lakes had to unload their cargo, which was later reloaded on the smaller canal boats, and the crop began to back-up in Buffalo. The resulting bottleneck required grain storage facilities to be built and grain elevators had to be invented. The grain elevators allowed for vertical storage that required a small footprint on the valuable property along the banks of the canal.

Grain elevators along the Erie Canal in Buffalo. *(Image courtesy of Library of Congress.)*

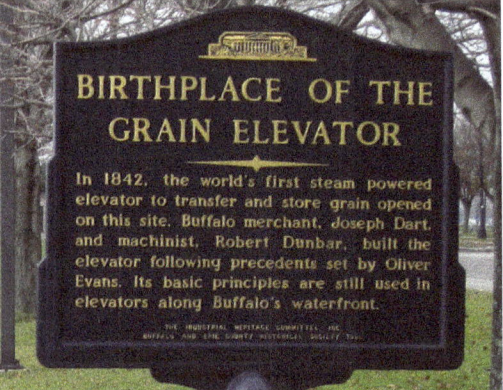

Historical marker along the Buffalo waterfront. *(Image source: Wikimedia Commons.)*

Tempered Drill Bits

The Niagara Escarpment was too hard for the normal drill bits in use at the time. A reward of $100 was offered to anyone who could produce a better drill bit. A blacksmith named Botsford invented a highly-tempered drill bit with a star shape that was far superior to the normal drill bits, and which was capable of drilling holes in the hard limestone escarpment. Holes were drilled and the blasting powder inserted to help continue the canal through the escarpment.

Stump Puller

The Erie Canal was built through forests along the route and the trees had to be felled and the stumps removed in order for the canal to be dug. A normal work crew of men could only clear four or five stumps per day. Crews designed a device with 18 foot wheels that used leverage to pull stumps easily so that a crew of six men and one team of horses could pull thirty to forty stumps per day.

Illustration of a stump puller, from a mural along the Erie Canal near Greece, N.Y. *(See copyright page for information about this illustration.)*

Hydraulic Cement

While studying the canals in England, Canvass White (see page 73) observed the type of cement being used. However, it was too expensive to import so he invented his own formula for the type of cement that hardens under water. He was granted a patent in 1820 but was never compensated for it, despite its widespread use in the canal.

Appendix 4:
The Erie Canal as Subject for Works of Art

There have been many works of art that depict the hard work it took to build the canal, the romance of travel, or scenes of canal life. Paintings were always a popular medium, as well as large murals inside buildings. A more recent trend, an offshoot of the tourism trade and recreational boating on today's canal, is the creation of large murals at ports and other locations of interest along the canal. The images below show some of this artwork.

"Tailing On" by Carlo J. Raineri. This painting depicts the Erie Canal in Durhamville. Between shifts, teams of draft animals were "tailed on" and "tailed off," meaning that workers held them by the tail as they were led on and off the canal boat. The original painting hangs in the Canastota Village Hall.

"Opening the Erie Canal" by Charles Yadley Turner, 1905. The two murals depict DeWit Clinton traveling down the Erie for the opening in 1825, and the "mixing of the waters" of Lake Erie and New York Harbor at the final celebration in New York. They are part of the collection of amazing murals in the DeWitt Clinton High School in New York City. *(Image source: New York City Department of Education.)*

Dawn Jordan is an artist who has painted several murals of the Erie Canal, including her recent work, "The Richmond Aqueduct." This mural won the Viewer's Choice Award at the 10th Annual Global Mural Conference held in Fairport, N.Y. in 2016.

"Port Byron N.Y." by Dawn Jordan. One of Dawn's largest murals is a 25' x 35' image of Tanner Dry Dock at former Erie Canal Lock 52 in Port Byron in the early 1900s. The artist was commissioned by the Lock 52 Historical Society and the mural was dedicated in 2005. She included her two sons in the foreground and a few of her ancestors in the boat.

"Weedsport N.Y." by Dawn Jordan. This 11' x 26' mural on the exterior of the Old Brutus Historical Society building depicts a location just down the road on Erie Drive in the early 1900s. The bridge connecting Brutus Street is long gone but several buildings can still be seen. Dawn Jordan was commissioned by local resident Jean Carrington and the mural was dedicated in 2007. Dawn included many of Jean's ancestors in the scene.

"2015 Wizard of Oz" by Dawn Jordan. Dawn's work reflects scenes from the Canal Era when travel was a 4 miles per hour pace on a smooth surface, as opposed to bumpy stage coach and horseback rides on unpaved roads. This mural, based on a painting by Edward L Henry (1841-1914), shows passengers in the finest attire riding comfortably on top of a packet boat on the Erie Canal. It is part of a three-mural triptych explaining "Canal Law."

Appendix 5:
Erie Canal Museums in New York State

There is no shortage of history along the canal today. Many local history museums have significant collections or permanent exhibits pertaining to the Eire Canal, such as the Buffalo Niagara Heritage Village, the Rochester Museum & Science Center, and the Albany Institute of History & Art. Indeed, some of the villages along the canal, like Palmyra, Fairport, and those in the Mohawk Valley, were established during the Canal Era and are living museums of that time and promote their canal heritage. The various welcome centers of today's canal system also provide historical information and are worth the visit. The mission of the museums given below is to primarily promote canal heritage, which is often depicted in their logos.

In 2016, the canal system witnessed two historic vessels on its waters. The Viking longboat, *Draken Harald Hårfagre*, sailed from Norway, down the St. Lawrence River, around the Great Lakes, down the Oswego Canal, east along the Erie Canal and Mohawk River into the Hudson, and south to New York City. It was met in Sylvan Beach by the *Hōkūle'a*, a double-hulled voyaging canoe that had sailed from Polynesia and into the Mohawk from the opposite direction. *(Photo courtesy of Richard Vang.)*

Erie Canal Discovery Center, Lockport

The Erie Canal Discovery Center is a new state-of-the-art interpretive center for the Erie Canal and the role that Lockport played in its history. It features Raphael Beck's mural, "The Opening of the Erie Canal, October 26, 1825." This floor-to-ceiling mural depicts the celebration surrounding Governor De-witt Clinton's ceremonial first passage through the now famous "Flight of Five" locks in Lockport to officially open the Erie Canal. Individuals from the painting come to life with the assistance of virtual-reality computer kiosks. A multidimensional orientation film transports the visitor back in time on board a recreation of the packet boat *Western Comet*.

Lockport is also the location of the Colonel William Bond/Jesse Hawley House. Hawley was an early advocate of the Erie Canal and was credited by Govenor DeWitt Clinton for making a believer of him in the project.

The Discovery Center is located at 24 Church Street in Lockport and online at *http://niagarahistory.org/discovery-center/*.

Spencerport Depot & Canal Museum

From 1908 to 1931, the depot was the only stop in Spencerport on the Rochester-Lockport-Buffalo interurban trolley line. The building fell into disrepair after the discontinuation of trolley service and it was moved and turned into a private home. In 2002, Maxine Davison bought and donated the building to the Village of Spencerport with the stipulation that the building "be used for the good of the community." On May 23, 2005, with the help of many volunteers, the building was moved to its current location on the Erie Canal.

The museum opened in 2007 to serve Erie Canal travelers and the local community as a museum, visitor center, and lending library. The museum houses collections related to the Erie Canal, transportation, communication, and local history on its main level. Downstairs there are restroom facilities for boaters traveling the Erie Canal.

Spencerport Depot & Canal Museum is located at 16 East Avenue in Spencerport and online at *http://www.spencerportdepot.com*.

Camillus Erie Canal Park

The Camillus Erie Canal Park has been under development since 1972. It is part of the Town of Camillus parks system. Within the park, every structure that is needed to operate a canal is represented: the remains of the original Erie Canal, the first enlargement, a replica of Sims' Store, a replica of a lock shanty, a canal feeder, Culvert 59, the Nine Mile Creek Aqueduct, and Gere Lock.

Sims' Museum is a replica of the original Sims' canal store, constructed by John Sims prior to 1860, which was located on the Erie Canal about two miles east of the present location. The original site was closer to Gere Lock and Belle Isle, able to take advantage of the fact that the boats had to stop there before entering the lock or stopping at Belle Isle. The store was stocked with anything the canal fleet needed in the way of medicines, cooking tools, food, water, kerosene, coal, apparel, hardware, and animal feed and equipment.

Camillus Erie Canal Park is located at 5750 Devoe Road in Camillus and on-line at *http://www.eriecanalcamillus.com*. *(Photo by Bob Reece, courtesy of the Park.)*

Erie Canal Museum

When the Erie Canal Museum opened its doors on October 25, 1962, it celebrated and preserved the life of the last remaining Weighlock Building in America. This Greek Revival building stands as a monument to the importance of the Erie Canal in the history of the United States.

A weigh lock weighs cargo boats to determine the tolls that were owed. Boats were weighed empty at the beginning of the season and then weighed again on each trip loaded with freight.

The museum collects and preserves canal material, champions an appreciation and understanding of Erie Canal history through educational programming and promotes an awareness of the canal's transforming effects on the past, present and future.

The Erie Canal Museum is located at 318 Erie Boulevard East in Syracuse- and online at *http://www.eriecanalmuseum.org*.

Chittenango Landing Canal Boat Museum

The Chittenango Landing Canal Boat Museum is located within the Old Erie Canal State Historic Park, fifteen miles east of Syracuse and north of the Village of Chittenango. During the nineteenth and twentieth centuries, cargo boats 96 feet long were built and repaired on this site. The museum tells of the construction of these boats, the workings of the restored dry docks, and the social history of the canal era.

The main feature of the museum is an excavated three-bay dry dock, with reconstructed miter and drop gates. Other features include excavated canal boat remains, model canal boats, a sunken canal boat which can be viewed when the water is clear, reconstructed woodworking and blacksmith shops, a sawmill, and the Enlarged Erie Canal towpath, which leads to a reconstructed aqueduct.

The Chittenango Landing Canal Boat Museum is located at 717 Lakeport Road in Chittenango and online at *http://www.clcbm.org*.

Canastota Canal Town Museum

Once a bakery and residence of the nineteenth century, the Canastota Canal Town Museum offers a history of the Erie Canal and brings to life local folklore and history. Located beside a remnant of the original canal, the museum is filled with authentic memorabilia, art, and other exhibits explaining Canastota's contributions to the canal, business, industry, sports, and agriculture.

Some exhibit highlights include an Outdoor National Park Service Wayside Exhibit, Canal Engineering and Canastota's Nathan Roberts, Life Along the Canal, Canastota's Lift Bridge and The Erie Canal, and Canastota's Industry and Commerce.

The illustration above is not actually a seal, but was created for a product in the museum shop.

The Canastota Canal Town Museum is located at 122 Canal Street in Canastota and online at *http://www.canastota-canal.com*.

Schoharie Crossing State Historic Site

For a canal boat to safely cross an intersecting shallow stream, the strategy was to dam it to create a pool of "slack water." But a creek or small river was often unpredictable in its strength and velocity, and the Schoharie Creek has always been notorious for flooding. Early on, the dam and some canal boats were lost trying to cross it during high water. The necessary alternative was to construct an aqueduct (1841) to carry the canal over the creek.

Ultimately, the Mohawk River itself was canalized and the aqueduct became unnecessary. Today, the Schoharie Crossing is a State Historic Site. Portions of the aqueduct remain, and the only two remaining locks of the original canal can be found there, as well as three enlarged canal locks and one barge canal lock. Putnam's Canal Store is also on site.

The Visitor Center is located at 129 Schoharie Street in Fort Hunter and on-line at *https://parks.ny.gov/historic-sites/27/details.aspx*. *(Photo courtesy of James Patrick Prendergast.)*

Waterford Historical Museum

The Waterford Historical Museum and Cultural Center is located in the 1830 Hugh White Homestead. The museum overlooks the Mohawk River and the old Champlain Canal and is also situated at the end of the Champlain Canal towpath walking trail.

The museum features local history including Waterford's unique role in the New York State Canal System. When visiting the museum you can see a working scale model of Old Champlain Canal Lock 4, and then visit the real lock located in front of the museum.

The museum is located at 2 Museum Lane in the Village of Waterford and online at *http://www.waterfordmuseum.com*. *(Photo by Marvin Bubie.)*

Appendix 6: Erie Canal Envy in the U.S.

The effect of the Erie Canal was among the most significant events in the country's history and astounded the nation. It was immediately recognized by everyone as the "Eighth Wonder of the World." All obstacles had been overcome by sheer brute determination and ingenuity. It seemed as if the young country could achieve anything it set its mind to.

Other states immediately saw the benefits to New York State and New York City and were determined not to be left behind. Several states began to build their own canals in a frenzy of expensive development. Pennsylvanians, aware that it cost more to transport goods 150 miles within their state than it did for New Yorkers to ship goods 750 miles between New York City and Ohio, spent $10 million to build a canal between Philadelphia and Pittsburgh, as well as a number of other canals throughout the state.

The states of Illinois, Indiana and Ohio launched projects to connect the Ohio and Mississippi Rivers to the Great Lakes. Illinois began the Illinois & Michigan Canal. Indiana began the Wabash & Erie Canal. Ohio began both the Ohio & Erie Canal as well as the Miami & Erie Canal. New Jersey, Maryland, and Connecticut all started building canals. By 1840, 3,326 miles of canals had been dug and completed without machinery, at a cost of $125 million. The Wabash & Erie Canal in Indiana was in fact 100 miles longer than the Erie Canal and the longest ever built in North America.

Some canals never even made it farther than paper planning, and although none were as successful as the Erie Canal, some were primarily responsible for the growth of other cities, such as Cleveland and Chicago. Most were soon eclipsed by the railroads, but several cities and towns were defined by the canals and, to some degree, still celebrate their canal heritage. Many have local museums dedicated to preserving that heritage through exhibits, photographs and canal boat rides. The National Canal Museum is located in Easton, Pennsylvania.

Shown on the following pages are the seals of the municipalities along the canals outside of New York State that have chosen to emphasize their canal heritage. Unfortunately, like some municipalities along the Erie Canal, a suitable image of the seal was not obtainable, and so not all have been included here.

Town of Avon
Connecticut

At the height of America's canal fever, the Connecticut State Legislature granted charters to private corporations for the construction of six canals in the state. Despite the enthusiasm of their promoters, four of these projects never raised sufficient funds to begin construction. Only the Farmington Canal (1822) and the Enfield Canal (1824) were eventually built. The most ambitious canal project undertaken in New England, the Farmington Canal extended from the tidewater in New Haven north to Granby, where the route continued into Massachusetts as the Hampshire & Hampden Canal, to a final destination at the Connecticut River in Northampton—a total distance of 80 miles.

The seal of the Town of Avon on the Farmington River displays a canal boat being towed by two mules.

Town of Plainville
Connecticut

Plainville, originally part of Farmington, was first settled about 1657 and incorporated as a separate town in July 1869. The name developed about 1830 from an earlier reference to the areas as the "Great Plain."

The industrial history of Plainville dates back to about 1828, following the opening of the Farmington Canal and the early industrial sites located in what is now the business section. Plainville had several shops that manufactured carriages which were sold and shipped all over the country, first by the canal to New Haven and then by larger sailing ships.

The seal has an illustration of gears, symbolizing industry, and a canal boat on the Farmington Canal, along with the motto, *ESTO PERPETUA*, which is translated as "Let it be perpetual."

Town of Windsor Locks
Connecticut

In response to the building of the Farmington Canal, prominent businessmen from Hartford formed the Hartford River Company to build a canal around the Enfield rapids. The canal opened in 1829 to much fanfare. Soon steam ships were carrying passengers from Hartford to Springfield. Among the notables was author Charles Dickens in 1847.

The Windsor Locks town seal features three circles in a trefoil form. Each of these circles depicts a mode of transportation that has served the town and is an inherent part of its history. One circle contains the Windsor Locks Canal, another an airplane (departing Bradley International Airport), and the third a locomotive.

City of Joliet
Illinois

The City of Joliet was founded in 1831 by settlers who were attracted to the area by the abundant fertile soil and the soft coal and limestone deposits. The geography of the area was marked by bluffs to the west of the Des Plaines River Valley, at the time well-timbered, and by gently rolling prairie.

After two unsuccessful attempts, Joliet was finally incorporated as a city in 1852. It initially prospered as a principal transportation corridor for both river and railroad traffic. With the emergence of Chicago as the dominant commercial center of the Midwest, a new network of heavily traveled routes developed. One of these was the Illinois & Michigan Canal, which was completed in 1848. Trade through the canal (and thus through Joliet) grew tremendously; by 1851, over $29 million a year in goods were shipped via the canal. This traffic spurred the growth of the city, which doubled in population between 1850 and 1855.

The seal has a boat in the upper right quadrant, symbolizing the I&M canal.

City of Lockport
Illinois

Illinois is the nation's most populous inland state. Its successful growth is due in large part to the Illinois & Michigan Canal, the first navigable link between the Great Lakes and the Illinois and Mississippi rivers. The canal was vital to the economic development and growth of the City of Chicago, the State of Illinois, and the rest of the Midwest.

The canal also fostered the growth of the small settlement that became the City of Lockport. Lockport thrived in its early days as the canal's headquarters and as an agricultural processing center. At the height of the canal's prosperity, its headquarters was second in importance in Illinois only to the state capitol building. In the canal's heyday, Lockport saw the construction of dozens of flour mills, grain warehouses and boatyards, as well as the creation of great amounts of wealth for savvy entrepreneurs.

Lockport was incorporated in 1853. The seal illustrates a packet boat.

Village of Seneca
Illinois

Incorporation was on February 16, 1865 for the Village of Crotty, named after Jeremiah Crotty, the founding father of what was to become Seneca. He first came to the LaSalle County area in the 1840s after securing a contract to build sections of the Illinois & Michigan Canal, which bisects the Village. In 1850, Crotty constructed his home on the old Abel Sprague claim adjacent to the canal, which became the first dwelling in "Crotty Town." With the 1850s came a railroad station (and station house) along the Chicago, Rock Island & Pacific rail line; a post office, store, blacksmith shop, and tavern; the first practicing physician and the first Catholic church; a warehouse and a steam elevator. The small town known as Crotty continued to flourish due to its location along the canal and railroad corridors.

The seal illustrates the canal, a bridge, and a historic Hogan grain elevator built for use on the canal in 1861-1862.

Will County
Illinois

Today Will County is gaining increasing national attention because of its standing as an Inland Port. Will County and its region have always benefited from major transportation infrastructure projects. The Illinois & Michigan Canal, which opened in 1848, connected the Great Lakes to the Mississippi River and the Gulf of Mexico, helping to establish the Chicago area as a major transportation center before the railroad age. Today the former canal traverses a good part of Will County as a park aligned along the towpaths by which mules pulled the canal boats. The sections of the canal between Lockport and LaSalle-Peru were designated as the first National Heritage Corridor in 1984 and include museums and beautifully restored canal buildings. The Illinois & Michigan Canal Museum is installed within the 1837 canal administration building in the aptly named Town of Lockport, itself laid out by the canal commissioners. The seal features the Illinois & Michigan Canal.

City of Delphi
Indiana

Delphi, Indiana, was first settled in 1824 by the Henry Robinson family. Delphi was formally established as a town in 1835 and incorporated as a city in 1866.

On February 22, 1832, the Wabash & Erie Canal was started in Fort Wayne, on the anniversary of George Washington's birthday. The Wabash & Erie Canal was completed from Fort Wayne to Delphi in 1840. The canal connected Delphi with Toledo by 1843, opening the area to commerce with the east. A July 4, 1843 grand opening celebrated its connection of Lafayette as the head of steamboat navigation on the Wabash, with Toledo, Ohio, on Lake Erie. The Toledo to Lafayette portion was in service longer than the southern section. Once completed, it connected Toledo and Evansville, Indiana. At 400 miles it was the longest canal in the country.

The Delphi seal depicts a canal boat being towed by a single mule.

Town of Montezuma
Indiana

The Town of Montezuma was settled in 1821 and was formally established in 1823. Although the origin of the name is not known, the name Montezuma was in the news in 1820 when the 94-mile middle section of the famous Erie Canal in New York was completed, connecting Utica to the Town of Montezuma on the Seneca River. Encouraged by that success, Indiana began the Wabash & Erie Canal project to connect Fort Wayne to the Ohio River. Montezuma became an important port on the canal and the turn-around basin. Warehouses and loading docks surrounded the basin, and passengers and area products were loaded and dispatched to New Orleans or the Great Lakes. Canal boats frequently spent the winter in the basin while they waited for the spring thaw. The canal started in the northern part of the state in 1836, had reached Lafayette by 1843, and by 1848, it had reached Montezuma.

The seal illustrates a canal with a packet boat being towed by a single mule.

Town of Chesapeake City
Maryland

The Town of Chesapeake City owes its existence to the Chesapeake & Delaware Canal. Begun in 1803, the 14-mile, hand-dug canal opened to traffic on October 17, 1829. The canal replaced the 300-mile ocean trip around the Delmarva Peninsula. As ship traffic through the canal increased, a little cluster of buildings grew into a busy commercial community providing goods and services. In 1839, the place was named Chesapeake City, prospering for the next 75 years. In 1927, the canal was dredged to a sea-level waterway, eliminating the need for ships to stop for the locks at Chesapeake City. The town's economic base quickly declined. Commerce was further complicated in 1942 when a ship destroyed the bridge that connected the two sides of the town and was not replaced until 1949. In the 1960s the canal was the third busiest in the world. The canal is now 450 feet wide and the busiest in the country. Chesapeake City is the only town in Maryland on a working commercial canal.

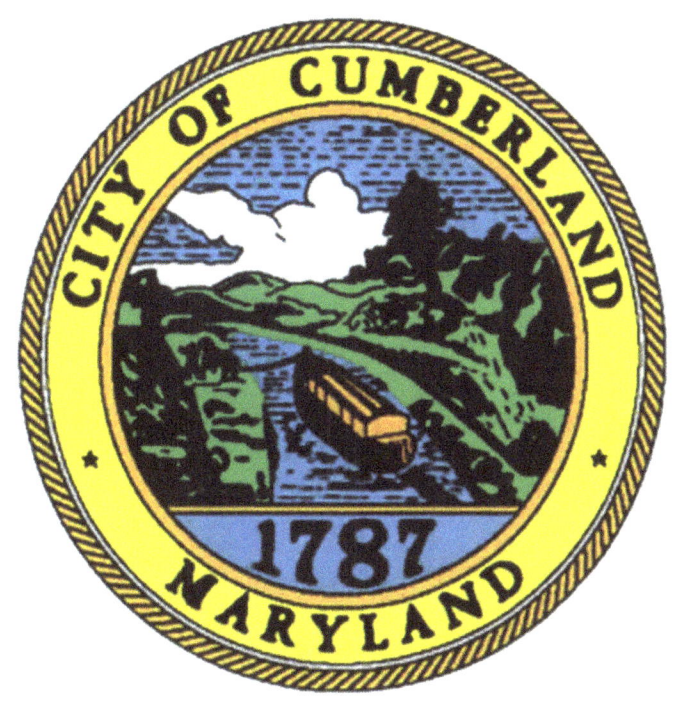

City of Cumberland
Maryland

George Washington has often been called the "Father of His Country," but he is also considered to be the "Father of the C&O Canal." During his lifetime Washington devoted much time and energy to the project of building a canal along the Potomac River.

In 1784, just after the Revolutionary War, Washington resumed his efforts to promote the canal. Now that he was a national hero, Maryland endorsed his plan. The Potowmack Canal Company was created in 1785 and Washington was chosen as its first President (see page 76). Eventually the Chesapeake & Ohio Canal Company acquired the Potowmack Canal Company and extended the canal to Cumberland in 1832.

The seal of the City of Cumberland has an illustration of a canal boat.

Town of Williamsport
Maryland

In 1787, Brigadier General Otho Holland Williams acquired the land and established Williamsport. He hoped the town would be chosen as the nation's capital by his friend and compatriot George Washington, who visited the site on October 14, 1794. The town was incorporated in 1823.

    The Chesapeake & Ohio Canal and the aqueduct were completed in 1834 and brought a boom of prosperity to Williamsport. Warehouses, shipping firms, saw mills and small factories were established, and town businesses and population expanded. Williamsport became a true canal town and its citizens earned the nickname of "River Rats." The C&O Canal is a vital part of the Town of Williamsport, which is home to many historical features such as Lock 44, the Lift Bridge, and the Conococheague Aqueduct. These features were modeled in the 1920s and Williamsport is the only location along the canal with all three of these historic features. The seal features the aqueduct.

Boonton Township
New Jersey

By 1800 the Boonton area had begun to grow. Conrad Hopler had not only built a forge, but had also constructed the first dam and bridge across the Rockaway River in Powerville. The later dam built by the Morris Canal and Banking Company flooded the area, creating a basin where canal boats could anchor for the night, load and unload, and dock for repairs. During the summer drought, this reservoir fed the canal through Guard Lock 11. The dam is constructed of concrete over a wooden interior. To enable mule drawn boats to cross the wide expanse of slack water, a bridge had to be constructed. One hundred seventy years after it was built, the center support stone pillar can still be seen today in the middle of the river.

The township seal illustrates this very unusual bridge with the stone pillar. Also featured is a plow symbolizing the importance of agriculture, and two picks remembering the mining of iron in the area.

Town of Dover

Town of Dover
New Jersey

The forging of iron became an important industry in Dover, and by 1800 Dover was clearly established as an industrial town, its success tied to the iron mines of the area and the production of iron goods. The location eventually became incorporated as a village in 1826 and as a town in 1869. It was during the time the Morris Canal was being dug that Dover was incorporated and the streets were laid out and named. The main street was named after one of the new forge owners from New York City, Joseph Blackwell. The canal was completed and in use by 1831, but was soon outclassed as a transportation mode when the Morris & Essex Railroad was completed in 1848. Eventually, Dover developed into a major commercial and industrial center with the completion of the Morris Canal and later the Lackawanna Railroad. The industries that defined Dover, and in particular, the Morris Canal, are historic sites now more than they are actual historic structures. The seal shows a packet boat and mule.

City of Lambertville
New Jersey

Settled in 1705, Lambertville is one of the oldest communities in Hunterdon County, New Jersey. This village grew into an industrial center with the development of the Delaware & Raritan Canal.

Some would say that Lambertville has changed little over the past one hundred years. Victorian houses and Federal row homes still grace the streets.

New Jersey's longest park, the Delaware & Raritan Canal State Park, runs through Lambertville, allowing the banks of the Delaware River to maintain their lush beauty.

The city seal has a canal boat being towed by mules in the center of the seal with a train and buildings behind it, and a farm scene in the foreground.

Borough of Stanhope
New Jersey

The Borough of Stanhope evolved from a small, late-eighteenthth century forge town to a sizeable iron manufacturing community in the nineteenth century. The Morris Canal, which flowed through the heart of the town, transformed Stanhope into a major outlet for canal goods into upper Sussex County. By the beginning of the twentieth century, the iron complex had been enlarged many times and was under the control of the Singer Manufacturing Company of Elizabeth, New Jersey. Although the iron manufacturing period at Stanhope was over by about 1925, numerous remnants of the early industrial community have survived the transition to suburbia.

The seal shows a canal boat exiting a lock, and iron mining tools.

Borough of Wharton
New Jersey

In 1831 the Morris Canal was completed between Newark and Phillipsburg, New Jersey, across the Delaware River from the terminus of the Lehigh Canal. On the way, it passed through Boonton, Dover, and Port Oram, all connected with iron. On this route it tapped the Morris County ore fields and became a carrier for both ore and pig iron. Its main purpose, however, was as an extension of the Lehigh Canal to furnish a route for anthracite from the Pennsylvania mines to the seacoast. Sites on the canal were selected for docks and industry—including iron works. Joseph Wharton acquired a large industrial empire that included the iron smelting in Wharton and the town was named after him in 1902. Joseph Wharton also endowed the Wharton School of the University of Pennsylvania.

City of Canal Fulton
Ohio

The Village of Milan, named after Milan, Italy, was the first settlement west of the Tuscarawas River in Stark County. The village, located on the present site of Canal Fulton, was platted on March 23, 1814. Ground was broken on July 4, 1825 for the construction of a canal connecting Lake Erie to the Ohio River. The route lay through Stark County and its construction produced 25 new villages between 1826 and 1836. The first was Fulton. In 1832, the name "Canal" was prefixed to Fulton as it seemed to convey a more dynamic quality. In 1853, Canal Fulton, West Fulton, and Milan merged to form one community.

The Ohio & Erie Canal was completed in 1832, at a cost of $4.7 million. It was the first important commercial avenue in the state. The census of 1840 reported that Stark County, as a direct result of the canal, was being transformed into one of the nation's greatest trade centers. The city's bicentennial seal has a packet boat being towed by two mules.

City of Canal Winchester
Ohio

When plans brought the canal through Reuben Dove's wheat field, he wanted to sue the state. The canal workmen convinced him that he would be better off laying out a town since the area was midway between two county seats, Columbus and Lancaster. On November 5, 1828, Reuben Dove and John Coleman recorded the first plat for Winchester, Ohio. Dove named the village for his father's hometown of Winchester, Virginia.

The Ohio & Erie Canal brought passengers, freight, and a means to transport grain to market. The village itself developed to provide the goods, services, and social opportunities for the people in the surrounding area. The first canal boat floated through Winchester in 1831. When the post office was established in 1841, the village name was changed to Canal Winchester, since there were five other towns named Winchester in Ohio at the time. On May 31, 1866, the Village of Canal Winchester was incorporated.

County of Coshocton
Ohio

In Coshocton County, Coshocton Lake Park has many miles of paved walking and bicycling trails. Commonly called "the Towpath," many of these trails follow the original towpath of the historic Ohio & Erie Canal. The trail connects Lake Park, Historic Roscoe Village, and the Monticello Canal Boat ride, and crosses over the Walhonding River via a rebuilt replica of the Aqueduct Bridge that carried the canal boats high above the river current. Other sites along the Towpath are Lock 27, the original sandstone canal boat locks which have since been turned into beautiful gardens, and two river basins that were once water sources for the canal.

The logo illustrates a canal boat against a stylized village silhouette.

City of Delphos
Ohio

On July 21, 1825, work began at Middletown on the western route of the canal that became known as the Miami & Erie Canal, which opened in 1845. It was 274 miles long and connected Lake Erie with the Ohio River.

The first settlers to Delphos were attracted by the work being done on the canal, most of whom were brought to the area as construction workers. The city was originally four little towns. In 1851 the four towns agreed to merge into a single town, called Delphos. It was famous as a major port along the Miami & Erie, with transshipment facilities for several major railroads.

By 1879, there were over a hundred factories churning out goods for the entire world, and even today the city enjoys an international reputation as a manufacturing center. By 1912, the city was connected to the rest of the United States by the first transcontinental paved highway, the Lincoln Highway.

The seal has a canal boat on the lower half.

City of Dover
Ohio

Dover was laid out in 1807. The town's first prosperity was stimulated by the construction of the Ohio & Erie Canal in the late 1820s. Warehouses were built and flour mills constructed. The only toll-collecting office in the county was situated in Dover.

Local industries included a woolen mill, blast furnaces, saw mills and tanneries. The city was always called Dover, but the post office was called "Canal Dover" for many years because of other Dover, Ohio, post offices. These were later abolished, and the Canal Dover Post Office became Dover on December 18, 1915. The town was incorporated in 1842. The importance of the canal began to decline in the 1880s due to the impact of the railroads.

The seal illustrates a view of the city with a tree and a canal boat in the foreground.

City of Logan
Ohio

Logan is the county seat of Hocking County, Ohio. Residents named the town in honor of Chief Logan, a Mingo Indian chief. Thomas Worthington established the community in 1816.

Logan grew slowly, isolated from much of the state by the Hocking Hills. In 1825, approximately 250 people resided in the town. By 1840, the number of residents increased to nearly 600. The principal reason for this growth was the completion of the Hocking Canal to the town in 1838. In 1840, Logan contained four stores and two churches.

The bicentennial seal celebrates the Mingo Indian chief for whom the town is named and the canal that brought growth and prosperity.

Village of New Bremen
Ohio

The building of the Miami & Erie Canal brought the first commercial work to New Bremen and opened a market for the products of agriculture. The opening of the canal was a day of festivity and rejoicing for New Bremen, which became a busy, bustling town. Hundreds of sixty- and eighty-ton freight boats traveled up and down the canal. Passenger boats carrying forty and fifty people made the trip to Cincinnati in a day and a night.

The New Bremen village seal was designed by Dan Keyes in 1997 and features the canal. The seal portrays the opened gates of the canal lock, with a boat coming through and the water gushing out. Behind this are the rays of the rising sun and the silhouette of a man with his left hand cupped to his mouth as if he is beckoning to others, his right arm on the canal gate as if to hold it open. The water is splashing up at the bottom of the seal and the founding date of 1833. The seal's motto, "Promise, Peace, Prosperity," is at the bottom.

County of Pike
Ohio

Pike County Ohio celebrated its 200th anniversary in 2015. From 1815 to 2015, the building of canals, railroads, the invention of electricity, several wars, the horseless carriage, and the Atomic Age all played a role in shaping Pike County.

At the beginning of the 19th century, Ohio was geographically isolated from the mainstream of economic vitality. The state was rich in natural resources, but inaccessible to the established eastern markets. The Ohio & Erie Canal changed that fact. Built in the 1820s and 1830s, the canal was carved from the wilderness to provide an invaluable link—from Lake Erie to the Ohio River—in the nation's transportation system, completing an inland water route between the East Coast and the Gulf of Mexico.

The Bicentennial seal features a canal boat on the Ohio Erie Canal, a sun rising in the background, crossed rifles that symbolize the early wilderness and a prosperous town on the left.

County of Summit
Ohio

In 1827 the Ohio & Erie Canal opened, helping the City of Akron to thrive. The canal flourished for forty years, spurring the development of commerce in the area.

Summit County derived its name from being the highest point on the canal and was originally known as "Portage Summit."

The Seal of Summit County was designed by history teacher George Seigman in 1981. It has an illustration of a canal boat in the lower right quadrant.

Village of Tuscarawas
Ohio

On July 4, 1825, at Licking Summit just south of Newark, Ohio Governor Jeremiah Morrow and New York Governor DeWitt Clinton, the man most responsible for New York's Erie Canal, turned over the first shovels of dirt for what would become the Ohio & Erie Canal.

In 1816, the Village of Tuscarawas was laid out from land that was owned by Eberhard Freytag and in the following years it grew with more annexed allotments. Not until 1825, when the canal was built through the village, did the town begin to attract settlers. *Tuscarawas*, for which the county, river and village are named, is an Indian word meaning "open mouth" or "mouth of the river."

The 1913 flood of the Tuscarawas River marked the end of the Canal Era for the area, as well as doing massive damage to the City of Dover. Pictures and memorabilia from the Canal Era and the flood can be viewed at Union Hall in Port Washington, Ohio. The seal shows a packet boat at Lock 15.

Village of Valley View
Ohio

On July 4th, 1827, the section of the Ohio & Erie Canal in this area was officially opened when a canal boat left Akron and proceeded through the locks to meet a welcoming boat, *The Pioneer*, six miles from Cleveland, and was escorted to the waiting village. The canal changed not only the landscape in the valley, but also the future economic and social development of the community and state. A new era of transportation had begun for the state of Ohio with new, undreamed of activity for the inland settlers. Local farmers and tradesmen found cash markets for crops and services, many contracted to work with their teams to construct the canal and then maintain it; others worked on locks and aqueducts, and built boats and repaired them. The valley's quiet atmosphere known by settlers disappeared under the new "canawlers" hauling freight and passengers on the busy canal.

    The seal shows a canal boat, a typical farm, and a modern high bridge.

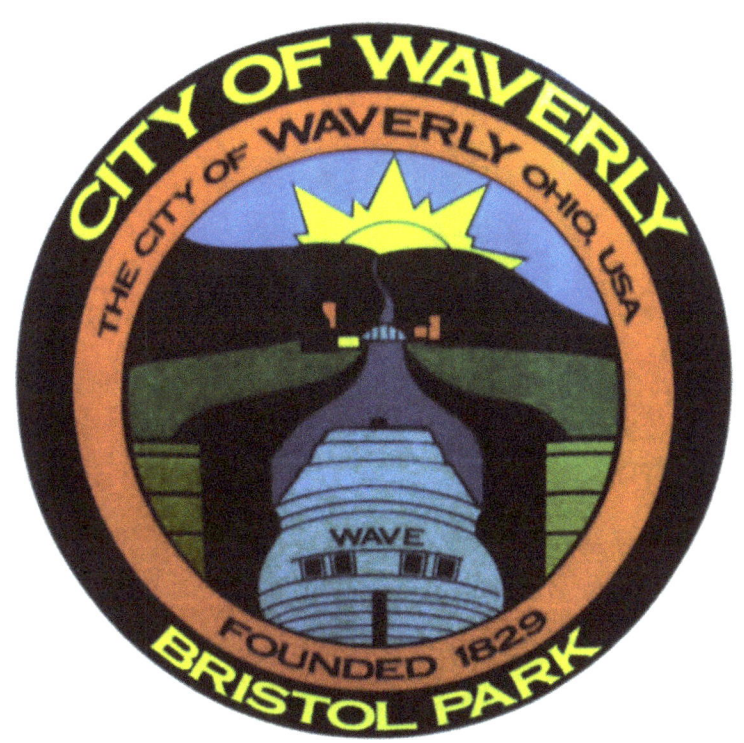

City of Waverly
Ohio

The City of Waverly was founded in 1829 along the Ohio & Erie Canal, which ran for more than 300 miles and connected Lake Erie to the Ohio River. The name of Waverly was suggested by an engineer on the canal, Francis Cleveland. Cleveland had been reading Sir Walter Scott's Waverly novels.

Waverly's growth was closely tied to commerce on the canal, and James Emmitt, the town's first entrepreneur, made most of his fortune from canal activities. He first hauled grain on the canal. He then built a grain mill, followed by a distillery to make whiskey. Emmitt added other businesses as well as many acres of farmlands. In the 1850s he claimed to be the Scioto Valley's first millionaire, reportedly was Pike County's largest taxpayer, and was said to employ half the men in Waverly.

The city seal is an illustration of a canal boat, the *Wave*, passing through a lock on its way through town.

Township of East Coventry
Pennsylvania

The Schuylkill Canal Navigation System, located along or adjacent to the Schuylkill River in the northern portion of East Coventry Township, was incorporated in 1815 and completed in 1824. The total length of the system was 108 miles. The purpose of the Schuylkill Canal was to provide a system for transporting coal, iron, lumber, merchandise and produce between the City of Philadelphia and Mt. Carbon and Mill Creek in Schuylkill County. It played an important role in the growth and development of East Coventry Township.

By 1870, the Schuylkill Canal became obsolete and eventually was abandoned in favor of other improved transportation systems. Between 1850 and 1950, there was little change or growth within the township. In appearance, it was still a rural community with agriculture as the dominant land use.

The bottom half of the seal shows a larger canal boat being towed by two draft horses with a rider.

Borough of Freemansburg
Pennsylvania

The Borough of Freemansburg was incorporated in January, 1856 and is approximately one square mile in size. Named after Jacob Freeman, whose grandfather settled the area in the 1700s, the borough has grown to a population of over 2,000 residents.

Nestled in the heart of the Lehigh Valley along the banks of the Lehigh River, a portion of the borough is located within the historic Delaware & Lehigh National Heritage Canal Corridor. Lock 44 of the canal is situated within the borough limits, along with the original Lock Keeper's House and the restored Mule Barn. Remains of the Geissinger Grist Mill are also located between the lock and the river. The borough maintains its portion of the Towpath Trail, which is an educational and scenic journey for residents and visitors alike.

Borough of Millerstown
Pennsylvania

Millerstown Borough is scenically set in the rolling hills of Perry County on the eastern bank of the Juniata River. The borough was incorporated February 12, 1849, and is the oldest town in Perry County, rich in historical lore.

The Pennsylvania Canal was begun in 1827 and the Juniata section was completed in 1832. Millerstown has had more old stone houses than any other town in the county, and many of them are still standing today as a beautiful monument to the quality of construction during those early years. Millerstown had sixty houses in 1825, and eighty in 1832. The stone "hotel" building on the west side of the square was built by John Wood in 1800. During the digging of the canal, there were seventeen hotels in town.

The seal has an illustration of a canal boat on the Pennsylvania Canal and the date of incorporation.

Borough of Muncy
Pennsylvania

Muncy is located along the West Branch of the Susquehanna River in North Central Pennsylvania. It was founded in 1797 and incorporated as a borough in 1826. The West Branch of the Pennsylvania Canal arrived in Muncy in 1834. Canals offered dramatically reduced costs for the transportation of goods and had an immediate influence on every community along the path, including Muncy. Private businessmen built the Muncy Cross Cut Canal in 1848 to take further advantage of the canal system. From the construction of the canal through the 1870s, Muncy grew and thrived. The canal, and later the railroads, helped to create an era of prosperity for its residents. Many architectural structures, including elegant homes, reflect the success of the community and can still be seen today.

The seal of Muncy is all about their history, and includes a canal boat and a reference to the Muncy Canal in the lower right quadrant.

Borough of New Brighton
Pennsylvania

In 1815, a plan of lots was laid out by two English engineers, the Constable brothers. For their work, they were granted the privilege of naming this new town, which they called Brighton, after their old home in England. The citizenry soon popularized the name to New Brighton, and as such, the new town was incorporated by an Act of Assembly in 1838.

New Brighton saw early prosperity with the opening of the Pennsylvania Canal in 1834. In two years manufacturing and industries in the area began to flourish, including flour mills, carriage works, foundries, a horseshoe-nail factory, lumber and paper mills, pottery works, a brick yard, a quarry, and glass companies. The success of these industries was due in large part to the abundance of water to furnish power, and the close proximity of New Brighton to the Ohio River for transporting finished products.

The seal has an illustration of a packet boat with passengers on the canal.

Borough of Shamokin Dam
Pennsylvania

Shamokin Dam was founded by George Keen in 1745. At the time it was named Keensville. Most of the residents were canal workers, raftsmen, shad fishermen, and eel fishermen. Restaurants and hotels provided support for the workers and travelers. A lock for the Pennsylvania Canal was located on the riverbank. Most of the local commerce at that time was revolving around transportation and supporting the canal.

Borough of Sharpsburg
Pennsylvania

The Borough of Sharpsburg received its charter on March 14, 1842.

Since its incorporation, Sharpsburg became an industrial town, manufacturing iron, brick, and glass. H.J. Heinz Company had its beginning in Sharpsburg.

One of the main reasons many companies migrated to Sharpsburg back in the 1800s was the Pennsylvania Canal System. Sharpsburg's canal was constructed by Phillip Miller in 1829. Goods were transported through the canal that bisected the borough, along with the Allegheny River.

The seal illustrates a canal with a boat being towed by two mules.

Borough of Watsontown
Pennsylvania

Watsontown is a borough located in Northumberland County, in central Pennsylvania. Situated along the West Branch of the Susquehanna River, the primary transportation route in the 1700s and 1800s, Watsontown grew as a transportation hub that spurred settlement and the building of mills and businesses.

In 1826 Pennsylvania authorized the creation of a canal system. Construction on the West Branch Canal through Watsontown began in 1828 and was completed from Northumberland to Muncy on October 2, 1830. The West Branch Canal formally opened on July 4, 1834. From the 1830s until the railroad was constructed in 1854, the West Branch Canal literally became the water highway for Watsontown. The canal had a major influence on the communities north and south of Watsontown.

The sesquicentennial seal shows a canal boat.

Acknowledgments

To make it easier for the reader, this list of source acknowledgments is arranged alphabetically by municipality, as opposed to the arrangement of the content within the book.

Since the First Edition of this book was published in 2010, the people listed here may no longer be in office. The author wishes to acknowledge their help with images or history or both.

State of New York

Albany, City of: John Marsolais, City Clerk; Archives of the Albany Institute of History and Art; Albany Public Library; the New York State Public Library.
Arcadia, Town of: *web.co.wayne.ny.us/office-of-the-county-historian/*.
Amsterdam, City of: Robert van Hasseln, City Historian.
Buffalo, City of: Paul Brown, City of Buffalo Print Shop.
Brockport, Village of: Leslie Ann Morelli, Village Clerk.
Canastota, Village of: Catherine E. Williams, Village Clerk.
Chittenango, Village of: Jill Doss, Village Clerk..
Clifton Park, Town of: Pat O'Donnell, Town Clerk.
Clyde, Town of: *clydeny.com*.
Clifton Park, Town of: Pat O'Donnell, Town Clerk.
Cohoes, City of: *www.cohoes.com*.
Elbridge, Village of: Jack Horner, Town of Elbridge Historian.
Fairport, Village of: *www.village.fairport.ny.com*.
Frankfort, Town of: Frankfort Free Library.
Fultonville, Village of: Kelly Yacobucci Farquhar, Montgomery County Historian/Records Management Officer.
Glenville, Town of: Joan Spencer Szablewski, Town Historian.
Greece, Town of: *greeceny.gov*.
Holley, Village of: Gail Sevor, Village Clerk.
Illion, Village of: Cindy Kennedy, Village Clerk; Mark Cushman, Mayor.
Jordan, Town of: *www.villageofjordan.org*.
Kendall, Town of: *www.townofkendall.com*.
Little Falls, City of: Kira Andrilla, City Clerk.
Liverpool, Village of: Mary Ellen Sims, Village Clerk.

Lockport, City of: Linda Groves, Secretary to the Mayor.
Lockport, Town of: *www.elockport.com*.
Lyons, Town of: *lyonstown.com*.
Macedon, Town of: *macedontown.net*.
Macedon, Village of: *www.villageofmacedon.org*.
Medina, Village of: *villagemedina.org*.
Menands, Village of: Kevin Franklin, Village Historian.
Middleport, Town of: Rebecca Schweigert, Town Clerk.
Montezuma, Town of: Cheryl Longyear, Town Historian.
Niagara County: *www.niagaracounty.com*.
Niskayuna, Town of: Helen Kopke, Town Clerk; History of Niskayuna, New York (Harder and Johnson, editors).
North Tonawanda, City of: *www.northtonawanda.org*.
Ogden, Town of: Carol Coeburn, Town Historian.
Oneida County: *www.ocgov.net*.
Palmyra, Town of: *palmyrany.com*.
Pendleton, Town of: *pendletonny.us*.
Perinton, Town of: *perinton.org*.
Pittsford, Village of: *www.villageofpittsford.org*.
Port Byron, Village of: Steve Johnson, Cayuga County I.T.
Ridgeway, Town of: *townridgeway.org*.
Rome, City of: *romeny.com*.
Rochester, City of: Danial Karin, City Clerk.
Rotterdam, Town of: Eunice Esposito, Town Clerk.
Town of Royalton: Jesse Bieber, Town Historian.
Schenectady, City of: *www.cityofschenectady.com*; *www.historicstockade.com*.
Schenectady, County of: *www.schenectadycounty.com*.
Spencerport, Village of: *vil.spencerport.ny.us*.
St Johnsville, Town of: *www.stjohnsville.com/Town.htm*.
Sylvan Beach, Town of: *villageofsylvanbeach.org*.
Syracuse, City of: *syrgov.net*.
Troy, City of: Donna Ned, Senior Planning Technician; Kathy Sheehan, Rensselaer County Historical Society.
Wayne, County of: *www.co.wayne.ny.us*

Other States

Connecticut
Avon, Town of: *www.avon.ct.com*.
Plainville, Town of: *www.plainvillect.com*.
Windsor Locks, Town of: *windsorhistoricalsociety.org*.

Illinios
Joliet, City of: *www.cityofjoliet.info*.
Lockport, City of: *www.cityoflockport.net*.
Seneca, Village of: *www.senecail.org*.
Will County: *www.willcountyillinios.com*.

Indiana
Delphi, City of: *www.cityofdelphi.org*.
Montezuma, Town of: *www.montezuma.in.gov*.

Maryland
Chesapeake City, Town of: *www.chesapeakecity.com*.
Cumberland, City of: *www.cumberland.gov*.
Williamsport, Town of: *www.williamsportmd.gov*.

New Jersey
Lambertville, City of: *www.lambertvillenj.org*.
Boonton Township: *www.boontontownship.org*.
Dover, Town of: *www.dover.nj.gov*.
Stanhope, Borough of: *www.stanhopenj.gov*.
Wharton, Borough of: *www.whartonnj.com*.

Ohio
Canal Fulton, City of: *www.cityofcanalfulton-oh.gov*.
Canal Winchester, City of: *www.canalwinchesterohio.gov*.
Coshocton, County of: *www.coshoctoncounty.net*.
Delphos, City of: *www.cityofdelphos.com*.
Dover, City of: *www.doverohio.com*.

Logan, City of: *www.loganohio.net*; *www.logan200.com*.
New Bremen, Village of: *www.newbremen.com*.
Pike, County of: *www.pikeohio200.com*.
Summit, County of: *co.summitoh.net*.
Tuscarawas, Village of: *www.tuscvg.org*.
Valley View, Village of: *www.valleyview.net*.
Waverly, City of: *www.cityofwaverly.net*.

Pennsylvania
East Coventry, Township of: *www.eastcoventry-pa.gov*.
Freemansburg, Borough of: *www.boroughoffreemansburg.org*.
Millerstown, Borough of: *www.millerstownpa.com*.
Muncy, Borough of: *www.muncyboro.org*; Bill Ramsey, Borough Manager.
New Brighton, Borough of: *www.newbrighton.org*.
Shamokin Dam, Borough of: *www.shamokindam.net*.
Sharpsburg, Borough of: *www.sharpsburgborough.com*.
Watsontown, Borough of: *www.mywatsontown.com*.

About the Author

Marvin Bubie was born and raised in the Capital District, graduating from Averill Park High School and Rensselaer Polytechnic Institute. He is retired from General Electric and has lived in New Jersey, Pennsylvania, Georgia, and Virginia. In addition, he served eighteen months in Germany with the U.S. Army in the 14th Armored Cavalry, and has returned to Europe many times visiting Switzerland, Italy, Austria, and Germany. Over the years he has collected the seals of various cities, towns, counties, boroughs, and villages in this country, as well as those in Europe. He has published two similar books, *On the Trail of Henry Hudson and Our Dutch Heritage Through the Municipal Seals in New York*, and *Celebrating the American Revolution: Municipal Symbols of a Free Country*, and is at work on another book of seals related to railroading heritage.

www.ingramcontent.com/pod-product-compliance
Lightning Source LLC
Chambersburg PA
CBHW080250170426
43192CB00014BA/2624